Worried about crime?

WORRIED ◊ABOUT◊ CRIME?

Constructive approaches to violence

◊Kit Kuperstock◊

Foreword by Will D. Campbell

HERALD PRESS
Scottdale, Pennsylvania
Kitchener, Ontario
1985

Library of Congress Cataloging in Publication Data
Kuperstock, Kit, 1929-
Worried about crime?

Bibliography: P.
1. Crime and criminals—United States—Case studies. 2. Juvenile delinquency—United States—Case studies. 3. Crime prevention—United States—Case studies. 4. Criminal justice, Administration of—United States—Case studies.
HV6789.K86 1985 364'.973 84-25150
ISBN 0-8361-3385-4 (pbk.)

WORRIED ABOUT CRIME?

Library of Congress Catalog Card Number: 84-25150
International Standard Book Number: 0-8361-3385-4
Printed in the United States of America
Design by David Hiebert

90 89 88 87 86 85 10 9 8 7 6 5 4 3 2 1

In memory of
Darlene
who never did realize
her dream of learning
to read because someone
shot her before her
glasses were ready

◊ CONTENTS ◊

◊ FOREWORD ◊

Prisons are always noisy. Just sheer racket! All the time. Daytime. Nighttime. I have been in them at three in the afternoon and three in the morning. The one thing that always strikes me is that there is never silence. Blatant verbal upheavals of caged animals, human animals whose born nature, like the nature of all animals, is to run free. Perpetual racket upsets me for it suggests that there is no peace there, an index of violence. Sometimes the hurting of confined frustration. Sometimes the screams of violence inflicted by guards or other prisoners. At other times the fearful cries of rape or internecine warfare. Inside prison walls there is always noise because prisons are places of violence.

But outside there is something even more telling: the wretched violence of silence. We have built the cages far enough from us that we do not have to smell the animals, see or hear them. So there is little to stimulate protest. If we do not think about them they do not exist. Save when one slips past the guards and out of the cage. There is existence then. At least until the animal has been safely returned to the coop. Safely for us.

For the sensitized Christian ear the spiritual clamor of that silence is more deafening than the din of the prison house. And that is what Kit Kuperstock's book is about. She breaks the silence and shouts vexingly from the cockcrowing void that we do shame to our own souls by what we do to those we lock up.

It is a very fine but very real theological line she draws and point she makes: the soul of the oppressor must concern us as much as the suffering of the oppressed. Yes, the criminal is the convicted oppressor and the victim is the oppressed. She makes that clear enough. But she also hammers home the often neglected point that in our cruelty we become the convicted (by God's judgment) oppressor and the criminal our victim.

In her own way she asks how long it has been since we visited one of the vile cages. And without casting stones she reminds us that however long it has been may be how long it has been since we have been in the presence of the one we call Lord. She is not as reckless and radical in breaking the silence as Isaiah, Jesus, or even Joan Baez. She does not proclaim release to all prisoners without condition as Isaiah and Jesus did. And she does not sing of razing the prisons to the ground in the fashion of Joan Baez. But her call is clarion.

No one can accuse her of ecclesiastical hemophilia. She is an experienced and hard-nosed realist who acknowledges early that some people must and will be isolated and confined. Though she questions, for reasons of economics as well as humanistic compassion and Christian commitment, the occasions leading to the vast numbers of those we lock up, she concedes that it will go on. The important point she makes is that for those of us in the household of faith, when it is culturally necessary for society to lock someone up it is not something we celebrate as righteousness. It is something we lament as our own shortcoming. We do not lock people up because that's the way Jesus, or Menno Simons, taught us to handle such people. We do it because we are afraid to do otherwise. Too often we offer a hearty amen to Caesar's action, rather than repent of our easy acquiescence.

We recall the New Testament observation that as we relate to Caesar's prisoners we relate to Jesus. We remember further that our own humanity is preserved insofar as we allow the humanity of the captive to be maintained. And also what Karl Barth told us years ago: that the first Christian community, the first church, was three criminals being executed by the state. All of them guilty. One of them Jesus.

Her concern is for all of us. It is for those locked up, those who lock them up, and those who have suffered the pain and indignity of violent assault, the loss of property or loved one. She sees us all as victims of something we have named crime. In answer to her book title, all of us are worried about the subject. Without presumptuous claim of panacea the writer skillfully and caringly offers some suggestions of remedy. Remedies pragmatic within the larger culture. Remedies also for the souls of those who would be faithful witnesses.

One remedy applying to both. There are approximately 341,000 organized congregations in this country. At some time during the year all of them will read or recite these words of Isaiah, the same words Jesus read at the time of his inaugural:

> The Spirit of the Lord God is upon me, because the Lord hath anointed me to preach good tidings unto the meek; he hath sent me to bind up the brokenhearted, to proclaim liberty to the captives, and the opening of the prison to them that are bound. . . .

Each year about the same number of men and women as there are congregations are released from prison. The majority of them will return as repeat offenders. What would happen if each congregation adopted the role model of Project Return, the organization for which the author works, and took one of those who is released (just one), offering the same fellowship, support, and hope they extend to all other communicants? Do we doubt that the recidivist rate would be drastically reduced? If we do, then we don't really believe what we say we believe.

And what would happen if each of the congregations took as their own just one of the 451,000 men and women remaining in prison, visiting them each week, bringing word from the free world to the prison, returning to the congregation with word from prison, hearing their story, telling them ours? Do we doubt that such a program would result in more prison reform than this nation has ever imagined?

No longer should we say we don't know what to do about crime. We know a lot. It is just that we go on relying on old remedies that have failed rather than trying anew the remedy the Lord revealed to us centuries ago.

In a manner seldom seen Kit Kuperstock subtly leads us through an exploration of our overall approach to *law*. "It's against the law." "Well, why is that which I have violated *law* in the first place?" In short, what is the criterion for the establishment of something as law? Is it as arbitrary as, "Thou shalt not break a cedar stick with a ball peen hammer?" Or are there rational human values behind each listing in the code? If that is the case, how consistent are we in legislating and cataloging the offenses?

I watched an exchange once between a masterful group leader and a Christian lawyer on the subject of law, crime, punishment, and grace. The group leader was a woman of unusual depth and commitment in theology and ethics. The attorney was a pietistic churchman of a large denomination. I knew them both but they did not know each other. She pursued a line of mercy, forgiveness, and reconciliation. He countered constantly with a hard-line legalistic argument that those who break the law should be made to pay their debt to society.

Without meaning to offend him she suggested that the group utilize the expertise of one trained in the law and try to reach consensus as to the basis of law. We discussed the first law of Scripture, God telling Adam and Eve not to eat from a particular tree. It seemed arbitrary, even capricious. She led us through the Ten Commandments. There seemed more practicality there but only two of them, killing and stealing, remain in today's criminal code. Unless the ninth be interpreted as perjury and the seventh as that rare prosecution for cohabitation.

I knew that our barrister brother had left his wife a year earlier and married another woman. It was all quite legal. I also knew that his eight-year-old son had reverted to temper tantrums and bed wetting, and an older daughter was in therapy from the scars of alienation and the bitter legal conflict she had watched unfold in a home she presumed happy and secure. I knew that, without meaning to, the leader was taking the lawyer into some unpleasant waters.

Our group had vowed to divest ourselves of all masks, facades, and deceptions. We discussed the subject for hours and from many angles, employing subgrouping, brainstorming, and various other group techniques. We finally decided that something becomes law if to commit it in some way hurts another person or oneself.

"Have any of you ever been divorced?" the leader asked. Several in the group indicated they had, including the lawyer. She went over and sat on the floor beside him. "Tell me about your divorce," she said to him, placing a gentle hand on his knee. "Were there any children?"

She presided, sometimes calm and soft, sometimes loud and harsh, as he described the enduring agony and resulting injuries his family had suffered. When it was over she walked over to a lectern, picked up a Bible, and then a state annotated code someone had brought into the room during the prolonged discussion. She came back to where he sat and dropped them at his feet. "Then why aren't you in jail, you rotten scoundrel?" she screamed. "You hurt somebody!"

When the sobbing was over she sat down beside him again. "Did I hurt you with that outburst?" she asked. The sadness in his uplifted eyes said that she had. "Yes. I hurt you," she continued. "So let's go together now and turn ourselves in. We're both guilty." And the hugging began.

If we take this book seriously we will be hurt too. Kit Kuperstock knows that and is sorry. It is evident on every page. What is also evident is that she will come to us and try to hug the hurt away. After reading her book I think I can hug her back. And some other people I would have had trouble hugging before.

Will D. Campbell
Mt. Juliet, Tennessee

◊ AUTHOR'S PREFACE ◊

Overcoming evil with good was never less in style. If someone strikes us on one cheek, we're expected to turn a can of Mace, a karate chop, or the handgun we keep handy for just such exigencies. On the international scene, the Pentagon and the Soviet military command continue their deadly spiral of keep up with the Joneses.

Crime, and fear of crime, are among the hottest political issues in the nation today (along with defense policy and fear of The Bomb).

Politicians sometimes actually win, or hang onto, their jobs with no promise more substantial than, "I'll be tougher on crime than my opponent." If they said they'd be *more effective* in reducing crime and in helping create a community in which fewer people hurt each other, the promise would mean something.

Crime hurts all of us: victims, offenders, agonized families of both, taxpayers, teenagers, owners of homes and businesses, old people, homeless transients. You. Me. We're frightened. Maybe really frightened about what seems to have gone wrong on our entire planet.

When we're frightened, we feel like being tough. We can

easily be talked into spending huge sums to build new prisons, lots of new prisons, and other expensive solutions to crime.

There are a couple of problems. The first is that the grand solutions rarely seem to do much good. The second is that when we spend all that money to punish people convicted of crimes, we can't use it for other things. Things like schools, job programs, medical care, housing, feeding people, and better and faster police work when a crime does occur. The irony is that research shows that those things *do* reduce crime.

Our grandmothers were fond of saying, "An ounce of prevention is worth a pound of cure." Prevention of crime would start with taking care of the million or so kids who are raising themselves on our city streets. By what legal means could they manage to stay alive? And when a young teenager is growing up without anyone to take care of him/her, what *is* the crime? Who is responsible?

We urgently need to find successful ways of caring for children whose parents are dead, or just not there. The things we are doing now rarely work very well.

Prevention of crime would also include taking a hard look at our casual use of handguns and alcohol. We'd have to reexamine the heresy that a person's worth equals the things that person *owns*. We'd have to take a very hard look at the violence that's so commonplace in our society that we rarely even notice it. We'd have to find useful, satisfying work in our high-tech society for the mentally and physically handicapped. We'd have to take a tough, analytical look at our drug problem and figure out how to make drugs less profitable for the unscrupulous, or easily tempted.

And when we haven't managed to *prevent* a crime, we need to decide how to deal with it. As human beings, as taxpayers, and especially as Christians, we find crime hard to handle. We have some pretty clear mandates about helping victims. (Ever meet anyone who *doesn't* know the story of the Good Samaritan?) When a crime is committed, we are apt to recognize "the least of these" (the victim, the dispossessed). In that same offender, we probably *also* recognize the evildoer, the oppressor, occasionally even the enemy (whom we are commanded to love).

So what can *we* do? Obviously it is futile (perhaps even foolish) to work on anything as massive as crime and criminal justice with simple, everyday tools: love, creativity, convictions about the value of persons and the cost-effective use of resources, and willingness to work very hard. Yet, scattered around the United States and Canada, are little clumps of people doing just that.

"The foolishness of God?" That would be a presumptuous judgment to make about these efforts. About, for example, Project Return, our small precariously funded agency in Nashville, Tennessee, which works with 700 people a year. Most of these are people leaving prison who need jobs and help in building good futures. We also work with families of people in prison. And, like other groups around the country, we've recently begun custom-designing sentences to be served *outside* prison. These usually involve restitution to the victim, tight supervision, community service, and upgrading personal skills.

Project Return is an intersection where many kinds of people work together to help make change possible. We sprout a lot of ideas, and some of them we've already had a chance to try.

From the Christian perspective, helping even one person make important changes is significant. Among the people we work with each year, a lot of important changes occur. These are significant to the individuals and in their impact on "the peace of our city." It has been conservatively estimated that, without Project Return (with an annual budget of only $70,000), at least 175 of the people who successfully put their lives together each year would be back in prison. (At a cost to taxpayers of about $2,000,000 a year!)

We are happy to save taxpayers money. We are taxpayers ourselves (when Project Return's fortunes are going that well!). But our main interest remains the individual.

Few things are as certain to give someone a healthy sense of humility as working with people who have committed crimes, with their victims, and with all the families involved and hurt.

With that hard-gained humility, I am sharing this book. Like

Project Return itself, it is a crazy quilt of cost analysis, street wisdom, theology, problem solving, grace, and laughter.

These are our ideas *at the present moment.* If you're already involved somewhere in the criminal justice area, we hope you'll find something useful and interesting to try out. You may also find something you disagree with. If so, we hope it opens dialogue that will give us all new ideas.

If you aren't yet personally involved, we hope you'll discover *your* way to help make change possible. Let us know if we can be of any help. Above all, share your discoveries with us.

◊ ◊ ◊ ◊ ◊ ◊ ◊

Names and sometimes small identifying details, of all prisoners and members of their families are changed. The only exception: well-known death row prisoners who seem beyond being harmed by further publicity.

The story at the beginning of chapter 13 originally appeared in *The Other Side* in a slightly different form as "Daily Miracle"; the ending paragraph of that chapter originally appeared in *alive now*.

My thanks to the Project Return staff and volunteers who have been an amazingly cheerful captive audience for supplying background, reading, and critiquing this manuscript: Pat McGeachy, Don Beisswenger, Nolan Eagan, Robert Arnold, Mamie Hammonds, Tara Seeley, Michele Munson, Ed Kuperstock, Ben Gaines, and especially, Harmony Wray, Bill Frith, and Bob Hill.

Kit Kuperstock
Nashville, Tennessee

◊ ONE ◊

If our child asks for bread and we give a stone— we'd better duck!

Many times before, I'd taken children to choose a puppy from a litter to become *their* puppy. Sometimes the choice was obviously love at first sight—sometimes, as with Timmy today, really difficult.

Yet when Timmy *did* choose and called forth his special pup, something significant happened. Moments before, the pup had been just a squirming member of the litter. Now he had been chosen. He was an individual. Almost at once, you could see the contrast with the others who had not yet been called and given their names.

This reminded me somehow of any service of dedicating a baby. Certainly we are not giving the baby to God. Before any human being knew it existed, this was God's child. We *are* dedicating the parents to their task, and the rest of us to participate in raising this child in love. But this, too, is really a celebration of something already in process. Before any baby reaches a celebration in a house of worship, there have usually been hundreds of hours of loving care.

"Naming the child" comes closest, perhaps, to describing what we're doing. But even the name is not conferred in a religious ritual, not any more. It was filed on a birth certificate the day the child was born, and some part of it, or a nickname, has been in daily use.

Putting that name and the attached vital statistics into government computers made a legal statement that the new child existed. A place would need to be ready in the public schools. Planners of roads, housing, and health care would need to take him/her into account.

We had a friend—Oskar, a Polish Jew—who was born in a cave to parents in the underground and never issued government identification. He was not a citizen. For years, he had no nationality, did not legally exist. Yet he was ceremonially circumcised, named, brought up in loving community, even under rough and difficult living circumstances. He had been welcomed and made a part of the community.

Some Christians celebrate this welcome by baptizing the baby. Those who wait for baptism until the child reaches a personally responsible age usually have some ceremony of welcome for a new baby. Nearly every human society makes some response to this need of the newborn child to be formally named and welcomed.

But what of the child whom no one lovingly names, no community celebrates? That child may be in peril.

The celebration doesn't have to take place in any church; it need not even be a formal ceremony. But it must occur and be sacramental enough, in the deepest sense, so the child is forever aware of being named and of belonging.

Bill Barnes, my pastor at Edgehill United Methodist Church in Nashville, Tennessee, says when he baptizes a baby, "This is a symbol of God's initiative—love given in advance before the child is old enough to understand or make an intentional response."

Although I love the service, I'm doubtful that *anything* is done to a baby without having impact and causing response, whether or not the child *intends* to respond.

Imprinting, the biological reaction of responding to and following their mother, occurs with ducklings the moment they emerge from the egg. In some form, it's found in the young of every known species in which parents nurture their young.

Even if something goes wrong and the mother is not there for the ducklings, imprinting still occurs. Young animals have been known to follow the first moving object they see: a person, a freight train, an animal with a wildly different lifestyle.

We all know that young humans are babies longer, and develop on a slower timetable, than other animals. Even so, I think it's reasonable to extrapolate that the naming ritual is important to the baby as well as to parents, older brothers and sisters, and other adults. It makes a dramatic statement of who he is and to whom he belongs, thus a prophecy of who he will become.

A few of the young adults who have come to Project Return from prison were named and celebrated as children. The great majority never were.

Fortunately, it's never too late for this name to be called, and this celebration to occur, but it does get much more difficult. If someone has reached the age of, say, 24, without ever being convinced of his or her unique value, it might require considerable effort—along with generous amounts of love and prayer.

Before any positive statements at all can be *heard,* much less internalized, some formidable barriers must nearly always be dissolved—a lifetime of statements of this person's *lack of value.*

The most emphatic statement of lack of value that the community can make is a criminal conviction. This is our formal declaration: *We will not tolerate this thing you have done* and with it usually goes the additional declaration: *We will not tolerate you. Therefore, we will lock you up in a prison located in a place we need never see.*

As the most extreme response, the community goes through a ritual killing (or delegates the unattractive task to be done discreetly out of sight) so that the person truly no longer lives among us.

This possibility of killing a person whom we have never even bothered to *name* is like finally getting around to aborting a 24-year-old fetus.

If your car is stolen, you'd be pretty safe to assume that the thief is not yet old enough to vote. There's better than a 50 percent chance that the burglar who breaks into your home or business is under 18. Vandalism and arson are also often kids' crimes.

Nearly everyone who commits serious crimes—felonies—was arrested the first time as a teenager. With the important exceptions of murder and white collar crime, serious crime is most apt to be committed by a young man of 15.

Juvenile delinquency isn't some kind of prelude to crime; juvenile delinquency *is* crime. After 16, our young man will probably commit illegal acts less often. By 25, crime is much less likely—by 36, really rare.*

What makes crime happen and how could we head it off in time? Let's take a close-up view of two young men I know well at Project Return. Both began criminal careers very early. Today both have become contributing citizens, law-respecting people. The only thing distinctive about them in a large group of young people who have committed serious crimes is that both of them are unusually bright.

Dale seemed simply to drift into crime. He was neither rich nor poor. At ten, he was unsupervised after school hours because his mother was dead, but his father tried to keep track of him. Their house was clean and located in a reasonably pleasant neighborhood. Some youngsters with Dale's potential have come out of such a childhood with a couple of college scholarships.

Unfortunately, that's not how it happened for Dale. Twenty years later he told me about it. He had been released from a California prison just a few months before. "I guess my father was strict, trying to make up for me not having a mother to ride herd on me. Anyway, I never seemed to have the same goodies as the other kids."

He was thrilled and amazed when, on his tenth birthday, his father came home with a shiny green bike.

---

*Ramsey Clark *Crime in America* (New York: Simon & Schuster, 1970), pp. 219-221.

"This isn't a gift," his father explained quickly. "I'm going to finance it for you. Better pay close attention," he added, for Dale had his eyes riveted on the front wheel he was spinning.

Obediently, he watched his father's face instead, and his father went on explaining. "I talked to the newspaper route manager and got a paper route for you. You'll start tomorrow, right after school. I'll expect a five-dollar bike payment each Friday after you finish collecting from your customers and pay your newspaper bill. This will teach you about business."

Dale, to keep that bike, would cheerfully have agreed to cut off one finger each Friday afternoon and give it to his father. He could already see the other kids' faces as he rode up, suddenly and miraculously one of the gang. He agreed so quickly and joyfully that his father felt one last warning was needed.

"Remember, now, those payments must be made on time. Five dollars each Friday at suppertime. It's high time you found out what a dollar's worth. First week you're late," he spoke slowly, hitting his palm with the other hand to emphasize each word, "that bike goes back."

Although ten is pretty young for a newspaper route, Dale did well until his customers started going on summer vacations. Then he'd often find they had forgotten to pay him and he'd have to wait until they got back.

The second week in June, it took him hours to collect even enough money for his newspaper bill, and at four-twenty on Friday evening, he was still 95 cents short of the five dollars for his father.

It occurred to him that one of the customers on vacation usually kept empty Coke bottles in the garage. He helped himself to a bike basket full, took them back to the store for a deposit, and got home a little late for supper, but with the full five dollars.

His father's frown about his lateness didn't bother Dale. Neither did taking the Coke bottles. He wouldn't have needed the old bottles if his customer had remembered to pay for his newspapers!

The next week, he discovered that several other customers

kept empty Coke bottles in their garages. He helped himself to some for spending money as well as enough to make up for whatever he was short for his bill.

In July, the weather turned sweltering and Dale got a bad sunburn. He hated every moment of his route with the handle of his bag cutting into his blistered shoulder.

One day, he abruptly decided it was easier to steal Coke bottles than to deliver newspapers. For a while he was terrified that his father would find out he had abandoned his route, but that never happened.

One week in August, he discovered that he had spent too much of his Coke bottle money that week. Less than an hour before suppertime, he was nearly two dollars short of the bike payment.

One neighbor who was out of town had left his garage door chained shut, so Dale hadn't checked that garage. Now, needing money badly, he decided it wouldn't be too hard to open.

Those rusty pliers he kept in his bike basket had come in handy before. It took longer than he'd figured to get the garage open though. And once inside, he found not a single Coke bottle.

Dale felt gypped. It was almost as if the neighbor had promised him the bottles he needed and then, after all that work, let him down. What now?

His father put their occasional empty Coke bottles under the kitchen sink. Maybe this neighbor did, too.

Crawling in the neighbor's high kitchen window proved much easier than opening the garage. It wasn't even locked, and Dale always had been a good climber.

There were a couple of Coke bottles under the sink, sure enough, but by the time Dale saw them, he was no longer interested. On the back of the kitchen cabinet was the biggest jar he had ever seen, nearly full of nickels and pennies someone had been saving. It was so heavy Dale could not crawl back out the kitchen window carrying it, so he unfastened the door instead.

It was fourteen years and three convictions later before Dale quit breaking into people's houses.

While Dale drifted into burglary by himself, Patrick, at 13, was hired and trained by an adult to be an armed robber.

Patrick, whose mother was in prison for dealing drugs, lived in an orphanage in the Irish Channel district of New Orleans. He had already outgrown an earlier orphanage. He was barely over five feet tall at 13, street wise, and a startlingly fast runner.

Working out with competitors for the Golden Gloves boxing championship, he attracted the interest of leaders of the Irish Channel Street Gang. After a little experience with him, they pointed him out to Jeff, a graduate of the gang, who had since put in six years in Louisiana State Penitentiary at Angola.

"Little and fast, huh?" Jeff mused. "Might be just what I need. That orphanage where he lives any problem?"

"Nah, they've got fire escapes. He comes and goes for us any hour we need him."

Eventually, Jeff recruited thirty young teenagers who he trained in small groups in the nearby bayous. The school the boys presumably attended had a back door; thus, both day and night operations were possible.

Besides Jeff's promise that they'd be making big bucks, the training itself was appealing to the boys: karate, marksmanship with a .38, stealing getaway cars, and cross-country and survival training. Jeff required a tough two-week training routine before he trusted any kid with a holdup.

Preparation for each job included stealing a car which could be abandoned as soon as you were safely away from the place you'd robbed. Jeff planned each job and coached the kids in detail. By sending the kids in to do the actual holdup, Jeff's risks were greatly reduced. If anyone had gotten arrested, it would have been a juvenile who would have received far less time than an adult sentence for armed robbery. However, as far as Patrick knows, neither Jeff nor any of the kids were arrested in two years of operation.

They robbed fast-food restaurants, supermarkets, and individuals making night deposits at the bank. Jeff kept most of the loot, but gave each kid a couple of hundred dollars from each job.

"Throwaway money," Patrick described it. "Some weeks I threw away $500." He used a lot of his crime money to take care of a teenage girl.

"Her family had kicked her out of the house. I set her up in an apartment, bought her an old Volkswagen, and sent her to school," he recalled.

"Did she help with the robberies?"

Patrick looked shocked. "Nope, nothing illegal. I was pretty strict with her."

Eventually, the orphanage became concerned about Patrick's truancy and sneaking out at night. One staff member, a former professional football player, was assigned to keep close track of him.

It was a futile assignment. It would have taken an agile and streetwise adult to keep up with a small, fast kid like Patrick in New Orleans streets and alleyways.

The New Orleans police never caught Patrick either. He was first arrested in Tennessee when he was 19, in an armed robbery with his mother.

Both stories have essentially happy endings. Dale and Patrick are each leading useful, satisfying lives today. Patrick, especially, uses his own experience as a tool for helping other youngsters toward more successful lives.

However, a great many people were terrified, and lost money and prized possessions as a result of these two youthful crime careers. No one was hurt physically—almost a miracle when you think of Patrick, as a young teenager, carrying around a .38. Still, I'm convinced that the whole unfortunate chapters could somehow have been prevented, saving their victims, and Dale and Patrick themselves, a lot of pain.

Yesterday, Daphne, 20 and just out of prison, talked to me about her juvenile crimes, runaways, and suicide attempts. "Nobody in the world *cared.* They sent me to halfway houses. I had a caseworker from juvenile court. A whole bunch of really smart people were supposed to be helping me and not one of them ever had time to listen. So *I* had a problem? Big deal!"

I suspect some of the people cared and, being professionally trained, listened. Obviously, though, none of them managed to communicate to Daphne that special quality of care and concern which is as essential to a child's growth as food and oxygen. Sometimes just one teacher or other adult who really cares, and communicates to the child that he cares, changes an entire future. Unfortunately, some young people grow up without ever connecting with that one essential adult.

All kids also need caring translated into practical things: a place to live, peanut butter, blue jeans, someone to see that they get to school regularly and on time.

We were startled to discover that 15 percent of the people who came to Project Return from prison had lost at least one parent by death before they entered their teens. By the time they were 15, about 18 percent had had at least one parent die.

Over half of the other people we work with, all convicted of at least one felony, grew up in foster homes, in institutions, or shuttled around from relative to relative. Many, who felt no one particularly wanted them, were supporting themselves on the streets by their early teens, occasionally even younger. They were not really runaways; their problem was that they had no place to run away from.

And, unfortunately, they were not unusual. It's estimated that nearly 2 million American youngsters simply disappear each year. Nobody's ever counted the street kids, but experts are reasonably sure that a large proportion of the disappearing 2 million wind up on the streets.

Any middle-class parent familiar with the struggle to keep voracious young teens fed, and the speed with which they outgrow shoes and jeans, usually reacts with shock to the idea of kids supporting themselves on the streets. "How do they stay alive?"

The one-word answer is, "Hustling."

Essentially a hustler, sometimes as young as ten or twelve,

knows his way around and can make quick contact with people. He will sell literally anything if he can get his hands on it, and he rapidly learns to. Drugs, stolen goods, and widely varied sex are the usual staples. If he hasn't already got what a customer wants, chances are he knows how to steal it, or fake it.

The sexist language is intentional. There is such a thing as a successful girl hustler. The one I know best is a very tough cookie indeed. However, she's one of a rare breed. Even a young male faces substantial hazards working the streets. A girl's smaller size, less strength, and greater vulnerability usually means she can't survive without protection.

And a girl usually has only one commodity that can be traded on the streets for survival, protection, and a roof over her head.

"I envy women who can get everything they have to have from just one man," a 19-year-old, who had raised herself on the streets, told me recently. "I've always had to have several just to stay alive."

Since I had been trying unsuccessfully to find safer housing for her than the rescue mission, with its huge population of winos, I didn't cast any stones.

Surrounded by adults who consider jail an everyday inconvenience, and closely watched by the downtown police, street kids are much more apt to be arrested than suburban youngsters. Since most street kids have no legal means of staying alive, they undoubtedly do get into more crime.

However, young people from rich sections of town are showing up in juvenile court for crimes as startling as burglary and armed robbery. Nearly all adults are working full time, and frequently divorce custody arrangements make supervision of youngsters even more haphazard. These presumably privileged kids often spend hours on their own, too.

Some acquire very expensive tastes: huge collections of electronics, records, and tapes; closets crammed with designer jeans; alcohol and illegal drugs; and hours after school (or instead of school) putting quarters into video games. To pay for these luxuries, and perhaps also from boredom, some kids turn to crime.

This hunger for things is carefully taught. Robert N. Bellah estimates that the average teenager has watched 350,000 television commercials before graduating from high school. Many of these same kids have observed adults going continually into debt to buy more and more goodies.

Even for rich kids, this is seductive. We're telling poor kids, We measure your worth by your possessions. So we're going to dangle all these goodies in front of you that you would have, too, if you were worth anything. But *you* can't have them. (Even so, I was really startled, as well as frightened, when a young man snatched my purse last summer.)

Children under 18 are supposed to be in the care of an adult. If parents are dead or missing, we try to put the child in a child care institution or foster home (usually a succession of foster homes).

Like successful prostitutes, successful foster children learn to be quickly friendly and agreeable, and not to expect too much of a relationship.

Pedro Santos got pretty good at it.

Pedro, despite his Hispanic name, is a slim rugged blond who looks at home in a Nordic ski sweater. By the time he turned eleven his German mother and Argentine father were both dead, leaving him in the United States with no relatives. Thus Pedro began the foster home circuit.

Since he was quiet and mannerly, with an engaging grin, Pedro quickly became a favorite of the social workers whose care and concern had to be spread over a whole group of youngsters. Foster families were also fond of Pedro. But one set of parents were transferred out of state. Another experienced serious illness in the family and had to have Pedro moved on.

By the third foster home, Pedro was pushing fifteen and like most teenagers was occasionally troublesome. His foster family was not happy when he skipped school and experimented with pot. The day he took a girl for a ride in their family car, with neither permission nor driver's license, that set of parents had had enough.

"Then they sent me to this church children's home with a real nice swimming pool," Pedro explained. "Church ladies think it's still an orphanage and take clothes out there for little kids. But really it's mostly for junior-grade hoods now. Like me," he added, grinning.

Actually Pedro hadn't gotten into more trouble than most of the older boys at the home. The close supervision made him restless, though, and he was happy to leave on his eighteenth birthday and try to make it on his own.

Two weeks later, Pedro and two other young men who'd also had too many beers were arrested breaking into a car.

One of the boys, slated to enter college that fall, had a father who knew how to intervene effectively. Promptly out on bond, he spent a strenuous summer working on an uncle's farm for punishment, and then had his record expunged by the court. Pedro and the other boy, fatherless, were still in jail awaiting their hearings when their friend left for college.

A few days before his hearing was finally scheduled, Pedro himself got a break. One of the counselors at the children's home, a special buddy of Pedro's, called Project Return. Bob Hill, our special projects director, agreed to go over to the jail and meet Pedro.

Bob waited patiently in the tiny, windowless conference room at the Old Jail until a guard finally brought Pedro and locked them in together. Shaking hands, the two young men looked each other over appraisingly.

"I got myself into a pretty dumb mess, didn't I?" Pedro said, smiling but wary.

Bob nodded, also smiling. Ten years older than Pedro, he is also tall and blond. From growing up in south Texas and a church job in Los Angeles, he probably knows more Spanish than Pedro does.

For the next couple of hours, Bob did a lot of listening, and got a few necessary items of specific information: Pedro's birth date, education and job experience, when his parents died, how he grew up, juvenile charges, and which teachers and counselors had been important in his life.

Back at the office, Bob talked to several of the people who had worked with Pedro over the years.

"I really like him, and he sounds to me like a good bet," Bob finally reported to me after all his research. "How about writing the judge that we'll find Pedro a job and generally ride herd on him?"

Since I'd long ago learned that Bob's judgment is nearly foolproof, I wrote a strong letter of advocacy for Pedro. With that much commitment from Project Return, the judge suspended sentencing for six weeks and ordered Pedro released the next day to start finding a job.

The next day was the Fourth of July, an appropriate day to walk out of jail, temporarily at least, a free man. Bob left a barbecue to go pick Pedro up.

Unless you have a family in town (in which case, you're probably not in jail), there's never any neat solution about where you spend the night when you get out, penniless. Since the Fourth of July weekend made it even more complicated than usual, Bob asked one of our volunteer families to put Pedro up overnight.

That family found him a pleasant and unobtrusive houseguest and he was allowed to stay nearly three months. He finally had to leave because the house was being remodeled and there was no place for him to sleep.

The job he needed also proved unexpectedly easy to get. Of all the people we've worked with, Pedro attracts jobs most easily. It's a valuable asset for a young man totally alone in the world. Considering his age and experience, he wasn't paid much (frequently minimum wage), but everyone he encountered seemed to want him to work in a restaurant kitchen, paint a sign, drive a truck, clean a swimming pool, or whatever.

Within a couple of days, Pedro had two full-time jobs—working in a lumberyard in daytime and as assistant cook in a restaurant on evening shift. He had court costs to pay before he went back for the postponed hearing.

The judge was pleased with Bob's report and gave Pedro a suspended sentence.

After leaving the volunteer's house, Pedro had moved into an apartment with some young men he had met at work, mostly Cuban refugees.

Less than a month later Bob received a phone call in the middle of the night from a clerk at the jail. He thought Project Return would want to know that Pedro had been arrested, along with half a dozen other young men.

At the jail, Bob heard a complicated story. When a group of people are arrested in the night, it's always complicated. There was a pleasant surprise, though. Everyone he talked to agreed that Pedro, for once, hadn't done a thing. He'd come home so tired from working the dinner shift that he'd slept through all the excitement.

Essentially a couple of young men, drunk or high on other drugs, had had car trouble just outside the apartment where Pedro and the others lived. From midnight on, they had knocked on the apartment door half a dozen times to borrow a tool or use the telephone. As their efforts to fix their car failed, they kept getting more frustrated and perhaps drunker. The last time they knocked, they forced their way in, a fight broke out, and neighbors called the police. Arriving at a mini-riot, police took everyone in sight to jail—including Pedro who went barefooted and yawning.

With a lawyer from the Public Defender's office, Bob had little trouble getting Pedro out. That time, at least.

Pedro is nearly nineteen, legally an adult. He's a nice kid, works hard, has reasonably good intentions, and that fortunate talent for getting jobs. What he lacks is family and solid neighborhood backing.

Pedro's experience with foster homes and orphanages seems about average. Occasionally, a particularly warm and generous family that enjoys children will get involved in foster parenting with outstanding success. A few of these are foster parents for years. They proudly show you graduation pictures of young people, sometimes dozens of young people, whose lives they have helped transform. They deserve a level of gratitude from the rest of us which we have not learned to express very well.

More often a family "likes kids" and "needs a little cash income."

Or people with more altruism than practical experience try foster parenting and find it too strenuous. The small stipends paid foster parents, usually a fraction of the cost of keeping the child in any institution, can't be much incentive. Some foster parents pay for extras like camp and music lessons out of their own pockets.

Some of the best foster parents have lived through the heartbreak of losing a child they have raised since babyhood and love as their own. Foster parents have traditionally been expected to provide a temporary haven without "getting attached to the child." The problem is that to develop properly, a child must have a permanent, predictable home with at least one parent, biological or not, to whom they become firmly and permanently attached.

Until recent budget cuts, a trend had begun toward better screening and continued support of foster parents. The occasional horror story seems to be mainly a failure in screening. In "The Man Who Keeps Going to Jail," John R. Erwin shared memories of foster homes of his childhood. And in "Uncle Frank's and Aunt Alice's" Uncle Frank sexually abused John's two younger sisters while Aunt Alice reacted with jealous violence.

Joseph Goldstein, Anna Freud, and Albert J. Solnit pointed out emphatically in *Beyond the Best Interest of the Child* that all children need to have a "forever" parent or guardian. Certainly, we need to help keep a close relationship going when a parent is temporarily in a hospital, prison, or a desperate financial crunch, and still trying desperately to work things out for the children.

Keeping children "on ice" while incompetent or indifferent parents make up their minds is something else again. As a matter of public policy, every child should be with permanent parents or guardians: biological or adoptive parents, other relatives who are eager to be permanent guardians, or permanent foster parents.

Since most of us today feel that homemade families must be limited to a child or two, adoption or long-term foster parenting is a responsible way to acquire a large and lively brood. We also need to keep a watchful eye on the laws and policies which have so much to do with the life chances of other children without families—and with crime.

◊ T W O ◊

Go directly to jail; you'll never pass go

No matter how complicated life became later, most of us can remember back to days of surprises from grandparents, playing with teddy bears, and being lovingly tucked in at night.

Heidi can't.

She was not quite two when rescuers found her crying in the wreckage of an automobile. Both her arms were broken. The adults in the car, including her mother who had been driving, were all unconscious from concussions and alcohol.

When Heidi was three, her mother stabbed her with a butcher knife in a drunken rage. An outraged juvenile judge ended parental rights, and sent Heidi to the children's psychiatric ward of a nationally known hospital to recover.

Heidi stayed in the hospital eight years. She claims to have learned to charm even the well-trained mental health staff. "They let me have anything I asked for. When I was finally transferred to a church orphanage when I was twelve, I was spoiled rotten."

In spite of her background, it's amazing how well Heidi functions today at 19.

Bright though she is, Heidi has largely avoided school. In the early days, she had too much turmoil inside to possibly sit quietly and learn multiplication tables. As she grew older, she was afraid she'd be laughed at if she tried to make up that early work she'd missed. The orphanage tried to enforce school attendance and other rules. Heidi ran away when she was fourteen, after two years of conflict.

Small and pretty, she encountered the hazards of the streets that one would, unfortunately, expect. More than once, she was gang raped. She also became addicted to heroin, supporting her habit by the usual casual theft, and consequently spent a few days in jail from time to time.

When Heidi was sixteen, she gave birth to David, now an eager toddler with curly red hair.

"I was an awful mother at first," she confesses today, but seeing her with her son makes you wonder about that. Certainly, there is an obvious and important bond between them. David loves everyone and learns effortlessly and continuously.

The other unusual thing about Heidi's story is that it ends on a hopeful note. About a year ago, she met a young man who had triumphed over a childhood as grim as her own. He had also served a prison term and knew he'd never serve another. Tough and caring, he insisted that Heidi get off drugs, and firmly stayed with her during several withdrawal episodes. She baked the cake herself for their wedding.

Heidi is now making plans to take cosmetology and dreams of eventually opening her own beauty shop.

"People feel good when they look good," she said defensively, when she announced her well-thought-out plan. (Apparently she feared that the rather academic Project Return staff would shanghai her off to graduate school somewhere!)

Heidi and her friends are lucky that she's alive to be planning a good future. The drunken assault with the knife might well have meant no future at all. Murder is the fifth leading cause of death among American children under seventeen.* Among young children, it is usually fatal child abuse by parents or caretakers.

**Causes of Death*, National Center for Health Statistics, Department of Health and Human Services, 1979.

The number of reported child abuse cases almost doubled between 1976 and 1980, according to the American Humane Association (413,000 in 1976; 789,000 in 1980). A higher percentage of cases was undoubtedly *reported* in 1980, because of public education and better legal protection, but there also appeared to be a considerable increase in the number of cases that actually occurred.

Child abuse comes in other forms, too. Hallie loaned her small son to the landlord to pay the overdue rent.

The rent was *very* overdue, three months, to be exact. The landlord said he was totally out of patience, about to turn Hallie and her three children out on the street. Then taking a look at her five-year-old Timmy, he added that he *did* enjoy kid sex. To get a time extension on the rent, Hallie turned Timmy over to the landlord for the weekend.

Although she has served prison time for other crimes, neither she nor the landlord was ever prosecuted for that one. Like the majority of crimes that occur within families, it was never reported.

Statistically, we are in more danger of assault, murder, and sexual abuse at home with our families than on presumably crime-ridden city streets.

Such crimes as incest and failure to support obviously occur, by definition, within families. Although incest is usually not reported, even the occasional known cases are enough to make social workers reluctant to have young girls in homes with stepfathers or fathers who drink.

One prisoner's wife, Bonnie, now 50, told me her father had *always* used her for a sexual plaything, apparently starting when she was a baby. It went on until, in high school, she abruptly managed to leave home and move in with a teacher's family.

"Mother must have known something was going on. She always treated me differently from my brothers and sisters, but she never did anything to help," Bonnie recalled, still amazed at the memory. "I felt like something out of a ragbag, until my second husband finally managed to show me there was nothing *I* could have done different."

Child abuse, tragically, is definitely a case of "the iniquity of the fathers being visited upon the children" quite possibly "unto the third or fourth generation." A child abuser is usually an abused child, grown to adult size if not noticeably adult otherwise. Those who were not physically abused as children were practically always neglected or subjected to severe psychological abuse.

Death, desertion, and divorce appear to damage families and the children growing up in them almost as much as crimes like theft and violence. When essential people just aren't there, essential things can't happen—like children growing up loved, cared for, and confident of their own value.

The society outside (us!) is not very good at giving families the support they must have to do their job. Some parts of that support are hard to quantify, even hard to describe. An intricate network of caring relationships and supportive services is needed.

But take something easy to quantify: money. Do you know what your state gives as an emergency living allowance to families with dependent children? In Tennessee, in 1984, it was $182.00 for a mother with four or more children. (Increased, in some cases only by food stamps, low rents in public housing, and Medicaid.) Tennessee was near the bottom; your state probably does better. But how much better? Look it up and try to figure how you would raise children decently on that amount.

Money is not always what's missing. It cost taxpayers a small fortune to keep Heidi in a well-staffed psychiatric unit for eight years. What her life might be like today without that expensive treatment we have no way of knowing.

But even after that huge investment, Heidi was on the streets by age 14. Care and supervision for a child, especially a teenager without an intact family, frequently just doesn't work. We badly need new ideas and practical research.

And we need them quickly. Those million or two runaways on American streets are 15, on the average, and they have no legal way to survive.

Folklore and literature suggest that there have always been a lot of kids among us who were either orphans or runaways. Remember Mark Twain's stories, and Horatio Alger's, and all the family histories about boys 12 to 16 heading West in the Gold Rush, or serving as soldiers in various wars?

Sometime before 1875 Charles Loring Brace wrote in *The Dangerous Classes of New York* about the "children of poverty and vice" who resented the rich. "Let the civilizing influences of American life fail to reach them," Brace concluded in alarm, "and . . . we should see an explosion from this class which might leave this city in ashes and blood."

I doubt if Mr. Brace and I would agree on many things, but his dire prediction might have been well-founded. Youngsters on their own have always found life especially difficult in cities. Today, most of us live in urban areas, and most existing jobs require considerable education and training. Child labor laws make it difficult for responsible employers to hire young teenagers. Job complexity and the minimum wage make it unappealing.

Most middle-class parents are convinced that their own children's futures depend on education and careful parenting. It is surprising how much more we expect of young people who have been less carefully taught.

Ricky, 15, had never known his father. Since his mother had recently been killed in a wreck, Ricky was sleeping on a cot on his grandaunt's back porch. His grandaunt, in her 80s, crippled and approaching senility, was quite unrestrained in telling everyone what a burden Ricky was to her. Even if she'd wished, she wasn't physically able to get him up in the morning and see that he left on time for school and his other appointments.

Ricky, in fact, had not been great about getting to school regularly and on time even when his mother was alive.

One morning, one of his teachers asked angrily, "Ricky, don't you people have a clock in the house?"

They didn't, though this was the first time Ricky had ever thought about it. Nothing he'd learned at home had prepared him for how excited some people get about time. He didn't bother to answer the teacher's question. No point in giving yet another proof of his family's inferiority.

By now, whatever sketchy order his mother had managed to put into Ricky's life had fallen apart. He intentionally stayed out every night until he was sure his grandaunt was finally asleep, and he rarely woke before noon.

Not surprisingly, he had recently been in juvenile court for several minor offenses. They would predictably get increasingly serious unless someone did some *very* good work, and quickly.

Jenny, his social worker, was trying. Concerned and experienced, with teenagers of her own, she kept working on possibilities for Ricky. Maybe the Job Corps. The frustrating thing was that Ricky usually missed the appointments she set up for him, or turned up very late with no sign of concern.

"Well," she told me, with the faintly humorous exasperation professionals sometimes show when talking about difficult clients, "tomorrow is Ricky's last chance. He *has* to be in the high school testing room by eight for a placement test he's already missed once—and I'm dreaming if I think he'll make it. His guidance counselor bought him an alarm clock out of her own pocket, but it hasn't helped enough that you'd notice."

"Look," I said slowly, "if this test is so important for Ricky's whole future, why don't I stop by his house and make sure he's up? Or I could send a young man, if you think that would work better."

"And if he *does* get in the program? Who's going to get him up every morning?" Jenny snorted. "I want a miracle for Ricky as badly as you do, but the first miracle is going to have to be that our boy learns a little responsibility."

I wanted to ask "And who's going to teach it?" but I work with Jenny a lot and didn't want our conversation to end on a heavy note. Instead we chatted, comparing notes as mothers will about our own kids and the summer that was just beginning.

"Tim—he's my 15-year-old—is the lucky one," Jenny said with evident pleasure. "He was chosen for a major Scout backpacking trip—leaves tomorrow for Colorado. In fact, I've got to clear up my desk and leave a little early to help him get his stuff packed. You know teenagers. Take your eyes off one for a minute and something goes wrong, even with the best of them—"

About that, at least, Jenny was correct. But a child who feels loved and competent is not likely to get into crime. This is especially true if wise guidance is there when he gets into mischief (as 100 percent of normal kids do). The guidance is to help the child understand why he doesn't want to repeat certain acts, and to help the surrounding community react firmly, but not destructively, to routine misbehavior.

When guidance *isn't* there, how helpful is the response from the surrounding community? It can be inferred from these vivid childhood memories reported by young adults leaving prison—memories of "wearing raggedy clothes and being teased"; "my mother's drinking and the kids calling her a whore"; "my father dying on my twelfth birthday"; and "being in juvenile court alone when I was 13, after a suicide attempt, because my 'ultra-religious' foster parents wouldn't be seen there."

It's a rare American who grows up without ever committing an illegal act. About 40 percent of American males are cited to juvenile court at least once. And in white collar crime, Charles E. Silberman pointed out, "well-bred people steal far larger sums than those lost through street crime."

But imagine for a moment that you're a young boy whose parents are dead, or just not there. Or you live in a foster home, or orphanage, or in a household headed by an overworked mother (and thus, automatically, are poor).

You are likely to have done something illegal when you were very young, probably six or seven (as is true of some of the men on the Project Return caseload). In the suburbs, you would be supervised well enough to be unlikely to get into real trouble. If you did, it would probably be handled by your parents and neighbors. At worst, the police would take you home and firmly request your parents to do a better job of watching you. That option isn't open to them, since there's probably no one to take you home *to*, so you'll probably make the first of many appearances in juvenile court.

The original wrist slappings from the judge will soon be replaced by short reform school sentences. If you are also abused at home, or made to feel worthless in school or juvenile institutions, your lawbreaking is likely to continue, with the crimes growing increasingly angry and violent.

Nobody will be particularly surprised and nobody is likely to give you any special breaks. You may graduate to an adult prison while you're still a minor by being convicted of a serious crime—armed robbery is the most likely. By the time you're 18, the community will have already had serious losses from your crimes and spent a lot of money keeping you locked up.

Since you began crime early and are short on family support, you will be classified as a bad risk for bond and special programs. Unless something within you causes dramatic changes, you have been programmed to be a criminal.

It sounds like *Brave New World* where babies were being methodically processed to be laborers, scientists, soldiers, and so on. Except, even in *Brave New World*, they had sense enough not to process their young to be criminals.

◊ T H R E E ◊

Serving time outside

Carol was 21 and pregnant when her husband, Lloyd, was suddenly arrested for car theft. Carol, a tiny redhead, with a laugh that bubbles through almost anything, was absolutely sure her husband wasn't guilty.

Since *he* was locked up, it seemed to be up to her to prove his innocence.

Carol and Lloyd already had two small children: Sharon, three, and Davey, more the size of a doll than a baby though he was 13 months old. He'd had to have major surgery right after birth and he could still digest only a special formula the doctor prescribed. But, like Sharon, he was bright and responsive.

Carol and Lloyd had solved the problem of Davey's care by working different shifts so one of them could always be with the children. After Lloyd's arrest, Carol could find no one she trusted to care for Davey. That ended her job *and* her paychecks.

The electricity was turned off first. She also received a final notice about the water bill, and the rental agency was threatening to evict them.

They'd gone to Memphis only a few months before to find work, and had no family or even close friends there.

"If we're going to starve," Carol said grimly, carefully counting her last 22 dollars, "let's go starve in Nashville so we'll be near enough to visit Lloyd."

She knew the conviction needed to be appealed, although she still didn't know how to go about filing an appeal. But it made sense that it would be easier in Nashville where the trial had been held.

Carol piled all their clothes and food (including one last case of Davey's expensive formula) and both the children into their old car. The car was mostly a Dodge. Lloyd, a talented mechanic, had built it from parts from wrecked cars, and it had cost very little.

During the 200-mile trip, Carol had to stop at roadside parks twice to do minor car repairs. ("I wasn't such a hot mechanic until I got broke. Then you learn.")

The food stamp office in Nashville told her about Project Return. Carol, by now nearly eight months pregnant, obviously couldn't get another job until after the baby was born. Although the family was eligible for Aid to Families with Dependent Children, the processing is slow and there'd be no income for at least several weeks.

Project Return telephoned several churches and explained the situation. Enough money was contributed for the family to survive frugally for a couple of months.

We were lucky enough at that time to have access to an apartment which prisoners' families could use for emergencies. Carol and her family stayed there for a couple of weeks. By then, we'd managed to get them into public housing by guaranteeing their temporary income.

The most surprising thing was a report from the lawyer to whom I had referred Carol. "I think one of Lloyd's relatives probably did steal this car," he said, "but I'm convinced this boy really is totally innocent. I believe I can put a tight case together, too."

"If the appellate court *does* find him innocent, I hope the family can collect some damages," someone said fervently when I told the staff about the phone call.

We saw a lot of Carol in the next few weeks. Occasionally, we'd keep Sharon at the office while her mother went for a doctor's appointment.

The baby was exasperatingly late in arriving. And Lloyd's appeal, like most appeals, seemed to take forever to go to court.

Just once, one sweltering August morning, Carol looked near tears. But by the time of our Prison Family Support Group picnic that night she was as bubbly as usual, helping all the kids roast marshmallows. When an older child went off the diving board for the first time, Carol led the applause.

Somebody persuaded an elderly aunt of Lloyd's to go to Nashville to visit him and take care of the children while Carol was having the baby. Although they'd talked over the telephone, it was the first time Carol and Aunt Margie had actually met. They rapidly became close friends and, to everyone's delight, Aunt Margie decided to stay and baby-sit so Carol could go back to work.

"I don't intend to live on AFDC a second longer than I simply have to," Carol had said firmly.

The baby finally arrived, cute, healthy, and three weeks later than expected. This created a problem. Davey had a medical appointment in Memphis for a major checkup when his new brother was only a week old. Since Carol didn't have a phone, I suggested she make the long-distance call from our office, postponing the appointment.

"I can't postpone it," she said. "This doctor's really hard to see and it's important about Davey."

She packed up Davey, Sharon, her 7-day-old son, and Aunt Margie and drove to Memphis for the day. She was tired, really tired, when they got back but glowing with the things the doctor had said about Davey's improvement.

"It's the first time Carol's ever been sure Davey would even live," Aunt Margie told us quietly. "The doctor says she's done miracles with that baby."

The day the new baby was two weeks old, Carol began a new job as a waitress. We protested, her doctor protested, but she persisted, and things seemed to go all right.

Carol is special, but it's surprising how many of the prisoners' wives we know are. There's no logical reason why prisoners should have especially attractive, spunky wives. We've finally decided that perhaps it's that only very special women stand by when their husbands are sent to prison.

I can understand why many wives feel it's more than they can handle. But my love and admiration goes out to the young women who are determined to hold their families together against such terrible odds. Even those legendary women who helped settle the American West didn't work as hard, or risk as much, as these prisoners' wives.

Although they can move around more freely, prisoners' families serve time as surely as the prisoner.

"They're convinced I'm trying to smuggle in either drugs or a hacksaw," an exasperated 70-year-old mother told me after a visit to her prisoner son. She was president of the missionary society in the small-town church she largely ran.

"It's bad enough having Leroy in prison but *I* haven't been selling any marijuana."

Everyone is searched before going inside a prison, but family members sometimes more thoroughly than anyone else. Although individual prison employees are often kind and helpful, the overall picture is that families are viewed with suspicion, and treated somewhat like prisoners themselves.

It was a really cold March day when I saw another mother in her 70s shivering outside the checkpoint door with other members of her family, all there for her son's parole hearing. They had already driven 200 miles that morning before arriving early for the nine o'clock hearings, and then they had to stand outside in near-freezing weather for nearly an hour.

There are benches around the walls in checkpoint, really a small entry office, and people routinely wait there until they can go back to see someone. But that day for some reason the checkpoint guards had decided that the families must wait outside.

Since the morning of a parole hearing doesn't seem a good

time to raise a fuss at a prison, I was silent, but it was hard. Having a prisoner in your family often means you'll find yourself herded around or made to wait outside—as if you weren't under painful stress to begin with.

It can get a lot worse. The worst I ever saw was when Joe Collette died in General Hospital all by himself, except for his guard, while his daughter was trying, as she had been for several days, to get permission to visit him.

The governor had already granted Joe executive clemency because he was seriously ill with a lung disease, and the prison doctor had asked Project Return to arrange his care. His only relative who had not given up on him completely was his 22-year-old daughter, Jenny.

Jenny's mother, remarried, would have been upset if she had realized Jenny visited her father twice each week. So would the rest of the family. They all hoped never to hear from him again. In all fairness, he had given them some very rough years.

I met Jenny for lunch to do some planning and was deeply impressed by this petite, pretty girl whose loyalty to her father had survived some bad times when she was growing up. He had been in a lot of trouble and served a lot of time.

"It's always when he's drinking," she said, worried. "How are we going to keep him from drinking?"

"By now, I don't think it could matter much," I assured her.

"I can take care of him weekends, clean up the apartment, do his grocery shopping and the laundry," she said, "but I don't get paid much."

"We'll manage the money," I assured her. "He's probably eligible for some kind of disability, and we can get some churches to help out at first. The hardest part will be finding him a place to live."

Housing would have been tough, even if Joe hadn't been on continuous oxygen. The doctor thought he could live in a small apartment for a while if people visited him every day, but his health, plus his record, sounded scary to landlords.

Jenny tried hard, and so did our whole staff, but we kept hitting blockades. We no longer had the emergency apartment and no agency in town would talk about housing until we had Joe out of prison and sitting in their office.

Finally in desperation, we asked Dismas House if they could possibly take Joe in. Dismas is a Catholic-run halfway house near Vanderbilt University, and a favorite ally. Although they had only one bedroom downstairs, where we already had 78-year-old John Davisson, and there'd be extra work for everyone, they didn't hesitate. Thursday night at supper they unanimously voted to take Joe in.

But Friday morning early Joe had a breathing crisis and was rushed (with a guard, of course) to General Hospital.

"I don't think he'll make it," the prison doctor said, sounding discouraged.

She did ask me to go see Joe and tell him there was a place waiting at Dismas. Hope occasionally creates miracles.

The associate warden for treatment thought he had arranged for me to visit on Saturday morning, and also for family members to visit, since Joe's condition was critical.

General Hospital is on the east side of Nashville and Tennessee State Prison is on the extreme west side. When I finally reached the hospital on Saturday morning, the guard said I'd have to have a written pass from prison security to see Joe. The guard, fully conscious of how sick Joe was, wasn't happy about the rules he had to enforce.

"It's been years since we've been allowed to let any visitor in without a written pass from prison security—and it's hard to get a pass. The family won't be able to visit until he's been in ten days—but I don't think he'll last ten days," he explained.

At my request, he telephoned the prison and talked to the head of security. The message: if I wanted to drive out to the prison, about an hour each way, they would talk to me about a possible pass.

I had other urgent appointments and it couldn't be done. "What about his daughter?" I asked.

"If she goes to the prison during office hours on Monday, she can possibly get a special pass," the guard said, shaking his head. "That's no way to treat folks when they're really sick," he added.

I wrote Joe a note about Dismas and the guard took it to him, possibly risking his job. He brought me a response from Joe and then delivered another round of notes. I gave Joe all the encouraging news I could think of and promised to see him somehow on Monday when the prison would again be fully staffed. His daughter was also going to see him on Monday, I told myself, if I had to go all the way to the governor to get permission.

But early Monday morning the guard walked into Joe's room from the hall and found him dead, still manacled to his hospital bed.

Not everything involving prison families is tragic. One of my favorite memories is Harris Cobb's clemency hearing.

His wife, Margaret, had kept the Prison Family Support Group going, sometimes almost single-handedly when everyone else was busy with emergencies. She had several teenagers by a previous marriage, and Harris' tiny son, whose birth obviously had some relationship to his work release. Harris had been in prison twelve years.

Margaret also had taken in a niece with a young child. Then one of Margaret's teenage daughters had found herself pregnant.

"That's a problem," Margaret had confided to me early in the pregnancy. "You don't want the girl to think it's okay to go get pregnant when she's not ready to take care of a baby—but the baby has to be really loved and wanted. If I can't get the right message across to everyone, I think it's most important that the baby feel welcomed."

I hugged her.

The baby did indeed feel welcome. How could anyone respond otherwise? She was adorable. Her entire big family, lots of neighbors and friends, and our staff lined up for chances to hold her.

Families always go to clemency and parole hearings and the

children are usually taken along, very starched and shiny. When it was Harris' time to meet the board, I knew I'd find Margaret with every one of her children, and probably with the niece and the two extra babies. But neighbors and friends come, too, as character witnesses, and Margaret had seen that Harris had plenty. The thing that fascinated me was that all these people also seemed to have small children, and all of them had brought them along.

I didn't know then—nor do I now—what magic Margaret had used to have so many little children looking so pretty and behaving so well. Any nursery school teacher would have been awed.

The parole board realized that *all* the children *couldn't* belong to Harris, but they couldn't figure out which ones did. There were an awful lot of children.

Quickly, one woman on the board, with a reputation for often asking tough questions, leaned toward the chairman and asked help in wording a motion. "I really think Mr. Cobb needs to be out as soon as we can possibly arrange it," she said, "to take care of those children."

Even with mothers like Carol or Margaret, prisoners' children are definitely victims of crime, and very innocent ones.

One very attractive young mother, Abigail, who took her two little daughters along to visit their father twice each week, told the girls, "Daddy is in the army."

("Boy," one of our staff members commented, "will those kids ever grow up to be pacifists!")

That bothered me at first. I have had all sorts of training in being straight with children.

Abigail spotted my concern and talked to me about it one day at lunch when the girls were in their kindergarten and first-grade classes. "How would you like to tell your children their father is serving time for rape in the state prison, and then turn them loose on a school playground?" she asked.

Explanations to children are tricky for most families. At our request, Martha Hickman recently wrote a charming book for five-to-eight-year-olds, *When Can Daddy Come Home?* which we hope will help (Abingdon, 1983).

Two inmates at Tennessee State Prison started a "Parents in Prison" project. Inmates study child development and learn how to be more successful parents. They eagerly write letters of advice to their wives. They try out their new skills on their own children, nieces, and nephews, and any other youngsters handy on the picnic grounds on visiting day.

When I see that group in action, I often think about a conversation with a first-grade teacher when our own children were small.

One of their playmates, Teddy, spent a lot of time at our house. We all enjoyed him. His mother was a single parent with two jobs and three children.

The teacher stopped me in the hall at school one day. "I've been wanting to thank you for taking such an interest in Teddy," she said.

"Poor little thing," she went on, concerned but certainly not professionally discreet. "Whatever we can do probably won't make much difference. He's a sweet child, but I'm afraid he doesn't have a chance. You see, his father is actually—" her voice dropped to a whisper "—in the penitentiary."

Whatever that teacher's mental picture of prison might have been, it didn't include prisoners eagerly attending classes to improve their skills with their children.

Only a minority of prisoners are women, but most of them have children. And women are far more likely than men to have been taking care of those children alone. When a woman is suddenly arrested, the children are probably placed in a foster home or institution, unless there are relatives to care for them. Occasionally, one of these children escapes the network entirely and hits the streets.

Children under eight can stay overnight with their mothers on weekends at Tennessee State Prison for Women. They have fun and everyone makes a big fuss over them. Only an occasional child is bothered by being locked in at night.

"It's the leaving that's hard," the mothers uniformly report. "I try not to cry, but my child always does."

A mother who is pregnant when she is sent to prison may have her baby delivered in a regular hospital instead of the prison hospital if she can afford to pay her guard's salary, plus the hospital bill.

If she's lucky, she'll have a mother or sister to take the baby home to raise. Otherwise, it goes into a foster home.

The mother and baby situations hurt. Pat McGeachy, president of the Project Return board for its first five years, also runs a special ministry to prison families. He arranges for young children to be brought to Nashville to visit their mothers in prison.

One day, Pat looked rather pale as he walked back into Downtown Presbyterian Church where he's pastor, and Project Return has free office space.

"What's wrong?" I asked, alarmed. Pat never appears shaken up.

"I just took a new baby away from his mother," he told me.

His role had actually been entirely helpful. He had paid the grandmother's bus fare to Nashville the day the baby was born, driven her to the hospital to visit a couple of times, and now had taken baby and grandmother to the bus station.

Considering her options, the mother was naturally grateful.

But, sure enough, Pat *had* had the job of taking that new baby out of its mother's arms.

I don't remember now why the mother was in prison but, looking back, I wonder if enough effort was made to find an alternative to locking her up.

There are certainly occasional parents who are abusive, unethical, or incompetent enough so their children are better off with almost anyone else. They are rare.

Both crime and prison can be very hard on families, especially when they are a long distance away. In the early days of

Project Return, we received a phone call from Mike Engle, a lawyer who worked for the Public Defender's Office then. He had a client, Paul Sullivan, in the workhouse with a broken jaw.

There were no special diets in the workhouse and no one was giving any thought to Paul, whose jaws were wired together. He had lost fifteen pounds and was becoming dehydrated.

We secured advice from a hospital dietitian and delivered a liquid diet to Paul. That solved the easiest part of his problems.

A Vietnam veteran, drawing disability for a psychiatric disorder, Paul had gotten himself locked up in the workhouse by exposing himself to a group of small children.

A bystander, with a long and unpleasant police record himself, expressed outrage by socking Paul hard enough to break his jaw. This gave the district attorney's office the urge to handle the situation quietly. They certainly didn't want that particular bystander to become a hero in the newspapers.

"Paul didn't touch a single child, and it doesn't sound too serious to me," an assistant district attorney told me, "but the children's parents are furious. The possible charges would carry long sentences, but I'd like to drop them if we could get him into a mental hospital. That's where he belongs."

That sounded simple and straightforward. *Except* we found that Veterans Administration hospitals were not taking patients with less than a 60 percent service-connected disability. Paul's was rated at 40 percent.

About that time, Paul's family in Mississippi heard from Mike Engle that we were working with him. They began calling and writing at least once a day. They also sent several checks to help pay for Paul's liquid diet.

His grandmother, obviously crying, told me over the phone, "You know, we've never even had a serious traffic offense in the family, and we just don't know how to handle this. We love Paul and we want to help, but we can't afford to come to Nashville for very long. Can you tell us what to do?"

I suggested that they contact every politician in their part of Mississippi and, sure enough, they eventually got Paul admitted to a hospital with a psychiatric ward not far from their home. We saw Paul off with great relief.

Sometimes realizing mental illness is involved helps a family accept a situation they can hardly believe, certainly not understand. Jewel Johnson's son appeared healthy enough, except he had been using drugs rather heavily. Jewel had known that, and suspected correctly that he was also selling them. She strongly disapproved.

Then things got much worse. I first heard about Jewel from her doctor.

"I have this patient who's having an extraordinarily hard time managing to visit her son in prison," he told us over the phone. "I wonder if you could give her some counseling?"

She came to the office the next day.

"They've got my son at Turney Center," she told me. "I've gone with my husband three different times to visit him, but I just plain can't make myself walk inside that place."

I mostly listened, expecting to find her problem was primarily embarrassment. It was painful for her even to talk about the things that had happened, and as she talked, her anger became obvious.

"It's not enough that Darryl was in an armed robbery," she said, furious. "He shot a man's arm off—his right arm. The man was an arc welder and he won't ever be able to work anymore."

She was crying now. "How could Darryl have done something like that?"

We talked a long time. I found it easy to understand her anger. I also learned that her doctor's concern was partly that she was developing high blood pressure and other stress-related illnesses.

"Is your husband visiting Darryl?" I asked finally.

She nodded. "He goes twice every week. I don't know how he does it, but he does."

"Darryl's not deserted then. I don't see any reason why you have to visit him until you want to. Except I wish you *would* go just one time to see where he is and what the place is like—and come back and tell me about it. Do you think you could? Just once—with your husband?"

"I can do anything once," she said, smiling faintly.

She didn't manage to walk inside that prison the next time she went, but she did the time after. Darryl was in a reasonably new prison for "youthful offenders." She was surprised at how clean it was, and that he was interested in some vocational education that was offered.

"How do you think he's feeling about the whole thing?" I asked the next time she visited me.

"We didn't talk about it," she said softly, for the first time without anger. "When he hugged me, he cried, though. Maybe things could change, like you said. You never can tell."

It was months before she visited him again but they did exchange a few letters. Finally, at the Prison Family Christmas party, Jewel told me she'd started going to the prison nearly every time her husband did.

"I hardly recognize my son. He's grown up some. He told me, 'You know, Mom, you can give someone else a kidney. Do you suppose there's any way you could give them an arm?' There isn't, of course," she added. "That hasn't changed."

Reality doesn't change, but slowly and painfully, we can sometimes learn to live with it.

Prisoners' families do more of this painful learning than most of the rest of us.

◊ F O U R ◊

The victim—who cares?

As a victim fled from a store during a holdup, he was fatally shot by a police officer. That was in Nashville, not long enough ago, and was obviously a tragic error. The police officer was fired.

However, it's not uncommon for victims to report feeling threatened not only by the crime, but by people responding to the crime. Police, courts, criminal justice system, even friends and neighbors often alternately ignore victims, or assume they somehow share responsibility for what happened to them.

When I was a college freshman, I was abruptly wakened one night by a frantic whisper from my roommate, Patty. Our beds were only about three feet apart, and I could see Patty's face, contorted by fright like Bette Davis in an old horror movie.

"Kit," she hissed. "There's a man in here with a flashlight and gun."

Could she be having a nightmare? Then I saw him, too. Our full-length window which led onto an upstairs porch was open behind him.

The intruder realized we were awake. "Pull those blankets up over your heads and don't make a sound," he ordered. "If you do, I'll shoot you through the heart."

Slight amusement at the melodramatic threat didn't reduce my terror. No danger of *my* making any sound. My throat muscles wouldn't have worked.

Patty, a Navy veteran, was less easily intimidated. "No sense dumping everything out," she said sharply, as the burglar rummaged through our bureau drawers.

In reply, he headed for her bed, his gun held straight out in front of him.

Not pausing to think, I grabbed a heavy bookend from my bedside table and threw it toward him. I doubt if it hit him, but the crash did give Patty and me the nerve to dash into the bathroom. We bolted the door and shoved ourselves against it hard, screaming "Help!" as loudly as we could.

People came running from all over the student center. Although the burglar had left, someone called the police. Our watches had been stolen, plus other jewelry, and Patty's billfold.

The police filled out a report, pointing out gloomily that there was no physical evidence. They were especially irritated because neither of us could describe the burglar. In the semidarkness, we'd seen little more detail than that he was considerably under six feet tall, and had carried a flashlight and a gun.

The next day a detective phoned the student center chaplain. There were so few useful leads that they were not going to investigate the burglary. The detective implied strongly that we had exaggerated our story. There had been a lot of burglaries reported in the university area lately, but no useful evidence in any of them.

"They could have said it wasn't important enough to assign anyone to without being insulting," Patty said angrily.

I could see her point, but I felt worse about a conference with the chaplain a couple of days later. Looking a little awkward, he called us into his study.

"The board asks that you please not discuss the break-in with the other students. They had an emergency meeting about it and, frankly, they don't want people to jump to the conclusion that they were negligent," he told us.

The things we'd lost didn't seem to be covered by anyone's insurance and were never replaced. And it was a couple of years before I could stay alone at night without real physical terror.

I suppose, though, it was a relatively inexpensive lesson in how you feel when you're a victim of crime.

More serious crime is also often not prosecuted. When you're working with the victim, you begin to understand why people sometimes have questions about our criminal laws. Someone was hurt, or suffered serious losses, and there's no real doubt about who did it. But proving it in court may be something else.

Claude had been a wild teenager, but stealing motorcycles and minor drug sales were the extent of his lawbreaking. He'd been in police court and briefly in jail. But as he grew older, things seemed to be going better.

Then, when he was in his mid-twenties, he borrowed his aunt's car for a date. Instead of returning it, he took off for California. He found a couple of her credit cards in the glove compartment and used them as he traveled, forging her name.

Since he was already a fugitive in a stolen car, it didn't seem to matter much what else he did. There were a few minor thefts along the way. Then he spent a night in a motel with a girl and left before she woke up, taking a $2500 cashier's check she'd had in her billfold.

He went across the border into Mexico a couple of times, hoping to find a really good deal on drugs, but nothing really worked out. By now the adventure was getting old. Every time he saw a police car, he got the heebie-jeebies. He decided to go back to Atlanta, where he'd started, and turn himself in. He had old girlfriends there who would probably give him shelter for the night and a sympathetic ear while he made plans.

One did, all right—a girl named Carol. She asked a lawyer friend to come over and give Claude some advice. The lawyer thought Claude ought to have a job before he turned himself in. "It would sure help in court," he pointed out, "and you'd have a better chance of being allowed to make bond."

Claude decided to spend the next couple of days job hunting. Then the lawyer would go with him to surrender to the police.

But tensed up as Claude was, he and Carol got into a fight. Still angry, he watched her drive off to work the next morning. Then he left, too. He took with him Carol's three boxes of jewelry. Some of the heirloom stuff was valuable.

When Carol came home and found both Claude and her jewelry missing, she was furious. She went straight to the criminal justice building to swear out a warrant for his arrest.

The judge shook his head. "Not enough evidence," he told her. "You have no way of knowing it was the young man who took your jewelry. It could have been someone else entirely. You can't prosecute with nothing but circumstantial evidence."

Months later, the stolen car was found deserted in another state. In the glove compartment was one of Carol's rings. Evidence at last!

One of the biggest controversies related to criminals is the question of bond. Under our constitution, someone charged with a crime is presumed innocent until found guilty. The stated purpose of bond is to assure the court that the accused will report for trial.

Making bond requires either 10 percent of the amount in cash, or owning real estate which can be put up for security. Even making a $2,000 bond, which isn't considered large, requires $200 cash, or ownership of real estate. Most people Project Return works with have no dream of owning real estate and $200 can seem an astronomical sum. A large bond, say $50,000, is hard for anyone to make.

Since we don't think people should be in jail who haven't been convicted of anything, we sometimes guarantee their court appearance. Or we can steer them to pretrial intervention, if they meet the guidelines. Sometimes we even put up the cash part of a small bond.

To keep someone locked up whom they consider dangerous,

judges occasionally set very high bonds. In certain serious cases, they also assume the discretion to refuse to set bond. This *preventive detention* of people not yet convicted of anything is argued about a lot. Certainly, it's potentially dangerous and needs watching.

We were more certain how we felt about it *before* the Sunday morning when I received a frantic phone call from Nicky. It was hard to understand her—I discovered later because her lips were cut and swollen—but she said something about Nat beating her up.

I thought I had misunderstood. Nat, who appeared happily married to someone else, impressed us as having done a great job of turning his life around. Since his release from prison two years before, he'd done a lot of volunteer speaking for Project Return. Recently, he'd begun talking about maybe finishing college and going to seminary.

I knew for a fact that he'd had a lot to do with other people finally building good lives. Nat's wife, Lucy, who had also served prison time, was equally determined that their future would be good. They had a reason—a baby daughter, Angela. Saying it was for Angela, they had gone into debt to rent a nice apartment and buy a rather impressive car. That was the only thing that had worried me before Nicky's phone call.

We'd all known that Nicky, who had worked the streets as a teenager, was too fond of Nat, but we'd figured it was one-sided.

"Better watch out for her," we'd warn, but we were kidding. We figured Nat had too much sense to allow himself to be compromised by a predatory and very young woman.

When I met Nicky at Shoneys restaurant half an hour after her phone call, I certainly didn't feel like kidding. She probably thought the dark glasses she was wearing hid her blackened eyes, but her whole head was bruised and swollen. On her neck I could see bruises, plainly made by hands that had tried to strangle her.

Nicky's hand shook as she tried to pick up her coffee cup. "I know you won't like this," she began hesitantly, "but I've been seeing Nat a little and we've had some—well, business dealings."

Something clicked. I suddenly understood those business dealings. Pimps beat up their girls sometimes, just to keep the other girls in line.

When Nat had shown up at Nicky's apartment very late the night before, she hadn't hesitated to let him in. "I didn't realize, though, how much he'd been drinking," she said. "I'm still not sure what I said that made him mad."

There it was again, that old myth that victims buy so readily: "What did *I* do wrong to upset him?" I didn't have time to be angry about it right then, though. Nicky discovered she couldn't read the menu because she was seeing double. Suddenly sick, she staggered and almost fell as she stood up to walk to the rest room. Supporting her with my arm, I steered her to my car and we headed for the emergency room.

The hospital admitted her to the neurosurgery ward. "She'll probably continue to get worse until the third day when her brain stops swelling," the doctor explained. "Until then, there's no way of knowing how bad this is. We'll keep her quiet and watch her closely."

The three days were terrible. Nicky seemed out of her head, vomited a lot, and was given continuous IVs. The bruises and swelling we could see kept getting worse.

"It's like that inside her brain case, too," the doctor said. "I'll be glad to give a medical statement for the court if she needs one."

When Nicky was finally a little better, I asked her about taking out a warrant for Nat.

"I can't," she said promptly. "If I got Nat in jail, and they let him out on bond, he'd kill me."

That seemed a reasonable fear. I checked to see if Nat was still on parole. The assault would certainly be a parole violation, and bond can't be made for parole violations. But Nat had recently been released from parole.

Could anyone promise Nicky in advance that Nat wouldn't be allowed to make bond? I checked around. No one really could, although I received conflicting advice from detectives, lawyers, and also from the district attorney's office.

"Nat's started drinking a lot, and he's involved with some other girls he'll probably hurt, too," Nicky said. "I'd like to do something, but it would be just like jumping off a bridge."

Her recovery was slow. Before she was out of the hospital, Nat and his family had left town. I don't know what happened to them.

Since Nicky got hurt, I've never been quite as sure about bond. The victim also has some constitutional rights—life, liberty, the pursuit of happiness. There are no easy answers. The longer you work in the criminal justice area, the more complicated even the questions get.

A person who commits a crime is regarded as owing a debt to *society*, rather than a car and $422 to the victim who lost them. The victim is largely ignored except when victim action is needed to "make a case." The victim may be suddenly asked by the police to take out a warrant, testify before the grand jury, identify stolen property, or appear in court. In between such requests, it's a fortunate victim who can find out what's going on.

This is even true when the crime is devastatingly more serious than stolen property. A member of Parents of Murdered Children gave this report: "We received progress reports at first, because one nice detective with the sheriff's department has been very compassionate and we called him many times. However, *we* had to do the calling; no one called us. Now the sheriff has ordered him not to give out any more information to us."

When police do communicate, victims are often confused about what they are supposed to do. The telephoned instruction, "Go swear out a warrant," sounds elementary to the police officer, but the victim rarely has a chance to ask "How?" What office in what building should he go to? What time of day? Will he need any particular papers? What will happen subsequently, and how soon?

Victims also feel frustrated because police just don't get very excited about one more burglary or stolen car.

One attorney remembers ruefully that when someone stole his sports car, police merely took a report by telephone. "We only have time to send officers out for physical attacks," the police switchboard explained.

Victims sometimes have a disturbing feeling that the cases chosen to prosecute are those that can be made quickly and easily, without spending much money. Extraditing someone from another state costs so much now that medium-weight crime has become relatively hazard free. The criminal just has to keep crossing state lines. Car theft becomes a federal offense when a state line is crossed, but the FBI rarely gets involved unless a car theft ring is operating.

Murder, rape, and usually armed robbery are prosecuted vigorously by all states. Federal crimes like bank robbery are prosecuted effectively by the FBI. Stolen cars are put on a nationwide computer. If the car is stopped for running a red light, or found illegally parked, the investigating officer may well discover that it's stolen.

But many people commit a series of crimes before anyone tries very hard to catch them, or prosecute them. Since they are mostly very young, this is unfortunate for everyone. It certainly creates a lot of victims.

If at all possible, we at Project Return seek alternatives to prison, and we think many situations can be handled informally. That's far different from encouraging a young person in the basic criminal attitude: I'm smarter than other people, so the rules don't apply to me.

The best news victims, and witnesses, have encountered in recent years are the victim-witness projects, usually under sponsorship of the district attorney's office. A knowledgeable advocate, often a volunteer, will go through the whole process with a victim, if necessary, explaining everything. If a hearing is postponed, the advocate tries to reach the victim by phone to save an unnecessary trip to the courthouse.

Victim-witness people respond to the human problems

found around any crime. Claire Drowata, who organized the victim-witness program in Nashville, recalls one Canadian girl who was with a young man who committed armed robbery. The girl did not even know the robbery occurred, but a good many women in that position have served prison time. Victim-witness advocates steered her through the legal swamp, and eventually helped her get back to her home in Canada.

Victim-witness specialists work especially with children who have to testify in incest or other abuse cases.

"There's sometimes a problem about that," Claire said. "You're afraid to send them home, and there really is no alternative."

She has found victims and offenders somewhat interchangeable. "A lot of them live in a dangerous world, and there often is neighborhood retaliation."

It's still on the drawing board but I would like to see some churches put together an Emergency Response to Victims program. As I visualize it, there would be a full-time staff member or two, knowledgeable about crisis counseling and community resources. One major staff job would be training volunteers from participating churches.

When a crime occurs, the police, a neighbor, or perhaps someone in the hospital emergency room, would call the Volunteer Emergency Response contact number. A staff member would look the situation over, help pinpoint the victim's immediate needs, and call in volunteers from the church nearest the victim's home. Victims we have known have needed doors repaired and locks replaced with more secure dead bolts, eyeglasses fixed, help filling out claims, and transportation to a doctor's office.

Victims of crime are most frequently older teenage boys, unemployed and frequently school dropouts. They are more likely to be black or Hispanic than white or of other races. While working with them in connection with a crime, some help with getting a job and planning a future would make a real difference.

The chances of being a crime victim go down steadily with age, despite the fear of crime that haunts so many senior citizens. However, on the relatively rare occasion when an old person is the victim, help is definitely needed.

A frightened old woman who lives alone may need, worse than anything else, a couple of sympathetic young people to spend the next two or three nights in sleeping bags on her living room floor. Or she might like to go to someone else's house for a few days, especially until her home has been secured again.

Victims with family, insurance, and both lawyer and minister quickly available, would probably not need this assistance. A lonely old person who lives alone might, even if there were no money problems. This kind of human, immediate response to crisis seems an appropriate role for churches. Faith communities should have both the love and flexibility that are needed. Fortunately, wherever there's a crisis, there's usually also a church within a few blocks.

That burglar I encountered in college was a frightening stranger. When people talk of crime and victims, they're usually thinking of crime by frightening strangers.

But actually the odds are as good, possibly even better, of your being the victin of a crime by a relative or acquaintance.

Two thirds of all murders are committed by someone who had a previous relationship with the victim.* Half of these are within families. Similar statistics are true for rape.

People turn up drunk and with guns at family Thanksgiving dinners, flimflam elderly aunts out of their life savings, even occasionally break into a relative's house or car.

The threat of the dangerous stranger is overestimated. Robbery is the only serious crime which typically occurs between strangers.

Spouses—usually wives—and elderly relatives are frequent victims of family assaults. After being taken for granted for

*Charles E. Silberman *Criminal Violence, Criminal Justice* (New York: Random House, 1979).

generations, wife battering has finally begun to disturb people even outside the family.

Caroline abruptly left home with three small children. Her husband's last beating had been too brutal. Since she was on probation for stealing an expensive bowl from an antique shop, she called her probation officer to report the change of address.

The probation officer asked Project Return's help.

"Caroline had never stolen a dime in her life before she took that bowl," she told us angrily. "Her kids were hungry. That husband! We know him well down here, and all his brothers, too."

Caroline's mother, pleasant, soft-spoken, and obviously sick, came to our office with her daughter and the children.

"We're staying with my folks," Caroline explained, "but they're really not allowed to have us. They live in the projects. We crowd them, too, real bad, and Mother's been awful sick."

"Cancer," her mother explained, sounding apologetic. "I just finished radiation treatments, and the doctor says it don't look so good. We certainly ought to be able to help our own daughter, but I don't see how exactly. My husband's on SSI because his heart's real bad."

Our whole staff spent hours on the telephone. Neither the Salvation Army nor the rescue mission could possibly make room for a woman with three children. Until income was arranged, which would take weeks, there was no hope of public housing.

Some of Project Return's friends occasionally take in a mother and child, or even two children, but they, too, regretfully shook their heads.

"There's simply no room in the inn," Mike Bailey reported grimly after we'd called everyone we could think of.

Caroline had been a good student and loved school before she'd dropped out at the beginning of her first pregnancy. I was getting all kinds of ideas about education for Caroline, and training for long-range good jobs. But immediate survival had to come first.

Caroline spent a couple more days with her parents, trying to hide three active children from the apartment manager. In the meantime, she got back the results from a pregnancy test: positive. At that, she gave up, took the children, and went back to her husband.

He beat her. Badly.

She was one of the reasons Church Women United and the YWCA opened a shelter for battered women in Nashville—but too late to help Caroline.

The most logical penalty for a crime is restitution to the victim. It's also the most biblical. Victim Offender Reconciliation Programs (VORP) began in 1975 in Elkhart, Indiana, and have spread to other parts of Indiana and Ohio. National news media and communities in other states have given considerable attention to these programs.

A meeting between victim and offender, with a trained mediator present, is the core of the VORP program. The offender and victim agree on restitution and repayment schedules.

There is always value to the victim in meeting the person who has had such a negative effect on his/her life. The "frightening stranger" perhaps turns out to be a young man who seems immature for 20, grew up in six different foster homes, and is eager to show off pictures of his new baby.

He is sheepish about meeting his victim. He was just thinking that selling some electronics was a quick way to get cash, not how important that stereo was to his music-loving victim. A chance to make restitution, instead of serving time in the workhouse, sounds good to him.

Many groups which put together alternatives to prison to submit to courts use some direct victim restitution.

Project Return has done a bit of that. However, we usually deal with relatively serious crimes. Courts and parole boards sometimes allow us to supervise someone in the community after fairly major crimes, if we put together an effective program and obviously know what we're doing.

We find that victims of serious crimes are usually reluctant to sit down with the offender, at least during the first few months after the crime. For one thing, the victim of a car theft or serious burglary may have spent thousands of dollars to move, change telephones to an unlisted number, and put in better locks and other security devices. The victim is terrified for fear the offender will come back and create more chaos in his/her life—perhaps, this time, hurt someone physically.

Besides being concerned about security, the victim may also just be exhausted—not feeling vindictive, particularly, but just not having the energy to handle anything else. Not yet.

This can change with time. It seems important that groups working with victims and offenders include some recent victims of crime in the planning processes. Some victims feel strongly that they don't want their addresses and phone numbers available from our office files—and we *have*, once or twice, found unauthorized people going through our files.

We have seen a young offender's genuinely good intentions melt temporarily as a result of alcohol or other drugs, and a group of other restless young people. A lot of crime looks like a high school feud except that weapons, alcohol and drugs, cars, and especially sex give serious adult consequences to the behavior.

For all these reasons, we feel that anyone attempting victim-offender negotiations needs to stay sensitive to the concerns of victims, and take them seriously.

It can be hard work but it's definitely worth doing. The victim not only receives restitution for losses, but sees the offender as perhaps an inept and unethical young human being who urgently needs some training and guidance, rather than a terrifying invader.

The offender has the chance to discover how he has harmed a real person. Offenders fool themselves a lot. One young man who stole a car convinced himself that the insurance company would buy the victim a brand-new one. Actually, though she received a fair enough payment, she won't be able to own another car anytime soon.

The most educational experience Project Return's people have had was Ruby Autry's armed robbery.

Ruby is the secretary for Downtown Presbyterian Church which gives Project Return free office space. She's about seventy, has a delightful sense of humor, and her office is just around the corner from ours. Everyone who comes to Project Return learns to know her, and like her a lot.

One day a man came to her outside office door, threatened her with a gun, and told her to get him five hundred dollars. Ruby headed for the church safe, but abruptly turned around the corner instead and darted into the Project Return office.

Half a dozen angry young men rushed into her office but the robber had fled, taking Ruby's purse.

"He'll drop it in the alley," George said. He'd served time himself for armed robbery. He rushed out, returning proudly in a few minutes with Ruby's handbag. Nothing was missing but her coin purse.

Everyone else was busy getting her coffee, watching for the police to arrive, designing a safer office door, and otherwise planning how to make such a dangerous intrusion impossible in the future. Seeing someone they liked as a victim had been a powerful lesson.

Of all victims, the family of someone who has been murdered suffer the most. The National Coalition Against the Death Penalty has recently begun listening empathetically to the families of murder victims, trying to learn ways they can work with these families. This is great news.

I remember being at a murder trial where the victim's family asked me what *they* had done wrong. All the ministers and distinguished professors were testifying for the defendant. (They were there testifying *against* the death penalty, but in the charged atmosphere of a murder trial, this can be a pretty subtle distinction.)

When a victim finds the ability to forgive, we can respond with awe and gratitude. We can't *expect* (certainly not *demand*) this forgiveness. Jesus said from the cross where he was being tortured to death, "Father, forgive them; for they know not what they do." That's the model for Christians. We don't, however, insist that our neighbors necessarily behave like the Son of God.

Forgiveness is a *gift* which makes it possible for the victim to laugh again, to eat and make plans, and lie down to sleep soundly in trust. Christians call it *grace*.

As Doris Donnelly of Princeton Theological Seminary said, "You reach a point where you realize you don't want to be in bondage to the person or event that hurt you. That realization can be freeing."

◊ F I V E ◊

Creating outlaws and media events

"The United States of America versus David Green—"

"*That* really made me feel outnumbered," David told me seven years later, after he'd been paroled from the federal penitentiary.

He'd been in his early twenties at the time of the trial, right back from fighting in Vietnam and being stationed with the army in Central America. The conviction had made him literally an outsider in his country—an outlaw. Because he'd become involved in importing large amounts of illegal drugs from Colombia, he'd been declared infamous and lost his right to vote.

I'm not questioning the *justice* of his punishment. But I do think we need to take a look at the message we give a young offender with our traditional statements in criminal law. All 227 million of *us* against him; that's really polarizing the situation!

Somehow this recalls that confession the prodigal son was putting together on his way back to his father's house: "I have sinned against heaven and before you; I am no longer worthy to be called your son."

His father had perfectly good grounds for agreeing with him. He could have cast him out, and for the record listed all his charges on some kind of notarized document. But you remember the story. The son was welcomed home so enthusiastically that he never had a chance to complete his carefully planned confession.

How did he turn out? Any recidivism? The story doesn't say, and I'm not really proposing that our judges start handing out fatted calves to defendants. (Although that *would* be cheaper, and conceivably as effective, as many responses to crime we're making now.)

I simply think we need to somehow communicate the message that whatever a young person has done, or could do, he belongs to us, we value him, and all 227 million of us have a stake in his future.

Let's take a close up look at ways we help shape that future.

What's the worst thing you ever did in your life? Give an insurance company or the Internal Revenue Service some exaggerated figures? Drive home from a party after too many drinks? Dramatically overdraw your checking account? Get some unauthorized help on an important exam or paper? Or could your wife or husband, or maybe your child, have made you so furious that you found yourself a bit abusive?

How would you like for a sensitive feature writer for the daily newspaper to do an in-depth piece on that worst thing you ever did, so all the readers will really understand how it was? No? Maybe it would work better to share publicly in church next Sunday? What would the effect on you be if everytime your name was mentioned or printed you were identified by that one lowest moment?

Everyone in prison wears, like an albatross around his neck, a constant identification based on the crime of which he was convicted. Even after serving his time, he'll be followed back into the free world by that damning label: "burglar," "bad check writer," "murderer," "forger," "armed robber," "child abuser," "drug pusher," "embezzler," or whatever.

For the rest of his life, he'll explain it to possible employers and landlords and other people he encounters who are important to him.

Devastating as the effect can be on people we take to court and lock up, our way of handling crime is still an alarmingly attractive model to some young losers. Let's take a look at Ralph, who because of his crime received the most attention anyone has given him in his life.

In the earliest days of Ralph's life, nobody responded when he cried. The grown-ups in his life were too occupied with their own problems (maybe plain survival) to have any energy left for the newcomer.

He did get diapered occasionally and someone sometimes stuck a bottle of milk, or Coca Cola, in his mouth. Certainly he was luckier than some babies whose parents have no loving memories of their own babyhoods. Although Ralph was handled fairly roughly sometimes, he never encountered actually bone-breaking abuse.

(Some recent fascinating research on the crying of young babies suggests that the cries of premature babies and sick babies are especially demanding. Such cries make anyone frantic to do *something*. Abusive parents are often those who don't know how to give their baby what he needs, or don't have it to give, and cannot stand to hear the crying.)

As Ralph grew out of babyhood, he finally learned to get occasional responses from other human beings. For him, temper tantrums or other dramatically bad behavior worked. Sometimes. Meanwhile, that hunger to have someone respond, someone acknowledge that he existed, kept growing inside Ralph, rampant as a cancerous growth.

Predictably, Ralph, who had never learned to be bright or charming, was not the child who got extra attention from teachers and the other children when he started school.

When tantrums and other childish misbehavior ceased to work for him, though, he might have learned a more powerful gambit: being able to threaten and frighten people. Or he might have just waited, a silent loner whom no one ever noticed.

Then there's the day he *is* noticed. Possibly he shoots a politician or erupts into other lethal violence that leaves some people dead, others distraught, and gets Ralph into front-page headlines.

One perceptive prisoner who was serving a life sentence for a rape twelve years before (his first and only crime) put it well. "When you commit a crime, you finally become someone special."

Even hours of police and courtroom questioning, painful though it sometimes gets, can still accomplish a lifetime goal for Ralph. For the first time ever, people listen eagerly to what he has to say.

And somewhere, listening, watching, another desperate, lonely kid gets the message. There is still a way to make them pay attention.

Besides the effect on the offender himself, newspaper headlines have a lot to do with the public's picture of crime and the people who commit crimes.

There's a paradox here. If a newspaper features the birth of a two-headed calf, people realize the story is reported because it's a rare occurrence. But when crime is headlined, people become convinced that it's all around us. Grandmothers huddle hungry in their apartments, afraid to walk alone to the corner grocery.

Everyone fears the threatening stranger, but it's questionable that that fear was really gleaned from media coverage. Anyone can flip through a daily newspaper and see how great a proportion of crime occurs in families and among acquaintances: "Stepfather Rapes Six-year-old," "Employee Plants Bomb in Car of Boss Who Fired Him," "Wife Tearful After Shooting Drunk Spouse," "Judge Rules Stealing Building Supplies Not Very Neighborly."

Statistically, you're in more danger of being attacked or murdered by your spouse or a romantic involvement, or having your billfold emptied or your car stolen by your own teenager, than you are of violence or theft from a stranger.

Most media have reported that the crime rate has finally begun dropping but few people seem to have noticed the small, academic-sounding stories. A reduction in crime rate doesn't have the front-page punch of a smoking gun, and TV camera crews can't photograph it at all.

Since I've had newspaper and radio staff jobs and have done lots of magazine writing, I'm partly talking to myself when I talk about the media. It would be hard, and require solid homework, but I seriously think news people could do a more responsible job of helping reduce crime in our communities. One important way would be in helping the public understand it and respond constructively.

The catch is (as they told us in journalism classes), bad news sells papers. Crime is news; people want to read about it. Are the giant headlines and catchy nicknames given criminals in a continuing story just routine coverage? (Remember "Son of Sam"?) Suppose journalists were convinced that front-page coverage was causing more crime? How much restraint would they, and should they, put on covering the news?

If one paper decided it would be responsible to play down most crime coverage, would a less concerned competitor be able to cut into its circulation?

Is keeping the public interested and informed of an ongoing series of crimes an effective help to police in catching criminals?

How do we balance the *protection* of press coverage with our concern about the invasion of privacy of innocent or vulnerable people?

Most of us are aware that the most carefully placed newspaper correction does not really erase the effect of a front-page news story. What will happen to the young man in a Southern city who was arrested for the murder, several years before, of a Girl Scout delivering cookies? After his parents spent thousands of dollars for defense attorneys, and the whole family had suffered trauma from which they can never recover, the district attorney made a public statement that he was convinced an injustice had been done, and that the boy was innocent.

In this instance the D.A.'s statement was prominently placed; it was news. But how well did it balance the columns and columns of speculation about the young man and details about his private life that had run earlier? Would *you* hire him for a baby-sitter? Would you go out with him?

How do we keep news about crime from causing more crime by people painfully hungry for attention—either the criminal currently making headlines, or the wistful young loser no one has noticed at all? There are theories that the "Son of Sam" coverage caused him to commit additional murders.

We've all read about notorious criminals who had all their press clippings with them when they were finally caught. Since it was probably impractical for them to subscribe to a clipping service, they had to put a fair amount of time and effort into collecting those stories and composite police pictures from lots of front pages.

A "big-time criminal," like a big-time entertainer, is most easily identified by the number of column inches he rates in the nation's newspapers and the amount of radio and TV time. By killing John F. Kennedy, Martin Luther King, all those Atlanta teenagers, or committing the Brink's robbery, people became big-time criminals, nationally infamous. It's a media definition.

People who are paid to reduce or punish crime, build prisons, or manufacture police guns and hardware, have self-interest in keeping us scared of crime. These include the people who keep and interpret crime statistics, and crime statistics make people willing to pay more each year for protection. (We might find something similar at the Pentagon.)

Then there's recidivism, the rate of return to prison after release. Anyone who has been in prison is far more likely to be caught if he does a crime, convicted if he's caught, and locked up if he's convicted. There are also technical violations which can return a parolee to prison—mainly not reporting to his parole officer on schedule which *is* serious, but not another crime.

Anytime someone who's already been in prison is charged with another crime, that's headlines. The majority of people who leave prison settle down and do well. They, of course, aren't news and, usually, desperately want not to be.

The prohibition on printing juvenile crime news is weakening, and perhaps it should. It has always varied, by both custom and statute, from newspaper to newspaper and locality to locality.

The first time a kid is in court for trivial shoplifting, or annoying a difficult neighbor, few newspapers would print his name. When there have been serious burglaries, though, we may feel that neighbors are entitled to know. The question is: Who makes the decisions?

The results of ambivalence about juvenile crime reporting can occasionally be surprising. The Oak Ridge, Tennessee, *Oak Ridger* headlined it on the front page when a 16-year-old boy fatally shot his girlfriend. When the case was tried in juvenile court, the outcome was never printed, though, since the *Oak Ridger* does not report juvenile court cases.

Another aspect of news reporting that should interest reporters and readers is the use of picturesque categories for minor, chronic offenders. You know the words: *police character, streetwalker, wino.* People in picturesque categories rarely can successfully sue for libel, but is that really all that's at stake?

Sure, there are salty-spoken streetwalkers who make good copy. I have a feeling that any reporter should know several pretty well before writing features that appear to take prostitution lightly. A high percentage of streetwalkers are the most lost little girl victims you could ever encounter.

Among other small-time criminals are a lot of people who are mentally ill, physically handicapped, or orphans who are raising themselves on the streets. Is it really "being soft on crime" to avoid making a police indictment the first thing for which they've ever gotten attention?

Nobody working in communications wants laws or judges interfering with the First Amendment right to keep people informed. Viewers and readers don't want their flow of information clogged up by the courts, either. I do think, though, that there's an industry obligation to keep crime in proportion, and frequently to resist the temptation to write a more dramatic story than this stupid act really deserves. By that very process, we may help make it also less frequent and less frightening.

There are also better uses of our free press than to put a person in an outlaw category from which he or she can never hope to climb out.

◊ S I X ◊

Alcohol and the other drugs

Ken had had only a few six-packs of beer in his whole life, half of them that Friday night. He'd felt like celebrating his brand-new driver's license.

Now the celebration was definitely over. There are few events less joyful than a teenager's funeral. Unless maybe it's talking to a teenager in jail who's just been indicted in the death of his best friend. Or the parents of either kid.

What started out as high school fun wound up in the morgue, in jail, and with a grand jury hearing ahead. Over half of *all* crime, like Ken's vehicular homicide, is alcohol related.

Surprisingly, the majority of people who get in trouble as a result of alcohol are pretty much like Ken. They're not alcoholics, or usually even heavy drinkers, according to a study published by the National Academy of Science in 1981.*

It's true that 10 percent of all the Americans who sometimes drink alcohol are classed as alcoholics or chronically heavy drinkers. Most of these are constantly in trouble as a result of their alcohol abuse.

---

*Moore, Mark, ed. *Alcohol and Public Policy: Beyond the Shadow of Prohibition* (National Academy of Sciences, 1981).

But they are so outnumbered by the 90 percent of light and moderate drinkers that these drinkers actually cause the larger share of alcohol-related crime and disaster.

Whenever a special effort is made to stop persons who are driving under the influence, 60 percent of those stopped will be normally responsible drinkers who did too much partying, according to the National Academy of Science report.

They need to be stopped, though. Behind the wheel of an automobile, a driver who is drunk from a rare evening's partying is just as deadly as the chronic drunk.

Besides tragedies like the one Ken caused, which are heartbreakingly frequent, there are the fights that begin with two guys each having a couple more drinks than usual. These are often prosecuted as assault, and sometimes even wind up as murder.

Or one of the men might instead have gone home and started abusing his wife. Or smashed out the window of a store he happened to pass. Or, with judgment temporarily impaired, he might even have been pulled into a group bent on burglary.

In a courtroom once, I listened to two parolees being sentenced to over three hundred years each for a brutal murder, kidnapping, and robbery. Their lawyer, desperately trying to put a defense together, tried *diminished responsibility*.

"Both of them had been drinking steadily, without eating, for over two days before the boy was killed," he told the court. "They've had problems with alcohol before."

Homeless winos, never voluntarily sober, are more apt to be crime victims since they really can't take care of themselves.

They are often among the public drunks which account for one third of all arrests. There are better ways to handle public drunks than putting them in jail. But however we deal with them, they make up a huge, expensive problem.

None of us likes to righteously tell other people what to do, but working in criminal justice makes one think hard about alcohol. The Bible tells us not to drink wine if it causes our brothers and sisters to stumble, an appropriate admonition for our society.

Drinking not only causes the nine million alcoholics in the United States to *stumble*, it often causes them to fall flat on their faces.

The illegal drugs cause crime by merely existing, since growing, manufacturing, selling, transporting, or using them is generally a criminal offense.

Most of the other drugs, like alcohol, are apt to become addictive. Your body reaches the point where it just plain won't work without its customary drug. If I don't have my morning coffee, I get a bad headache by midmorning, which suggests a caffeine addiction. I need to cut down on coffee but I also need to remember my own addiction when I'm working with someone else with substance abuse problems. "Judge not!"

Project Return has worked with several federal parolees who had served time for smuggling drugs into the United States from Central America. Their stories sound like James Bond, including the sudden deaths. Because I feel the Central American drug traffic has made colorful copy for entirely too many journalists already, I'm going to stick to statistics. Even the statistics are inevitably dramatic, however.

The United States gets the majority of its cocaine and marijuana from Colombia, as well as things like counterfeit Qualuudes. The drugs, although illegal in Colombia, are important to that nation's economy. Cocaine and marijuana add three billion dollars to Colombia's exports each year—greater than the total of all other exports combined, including coffee.

Although legalizing the drugs would give Colombia the ability to tax them, there seems to be no chance that will happen. There's an unlikely set of powerful opponents to that—the Roman Catholic Church, the governments of both the United States and Colombia, and the major drug dealers themselves who find the status quo exceedingly profitable.*

Coca, mostly grown in the Andes Mountains by Peruvian

---

*A major source used was a paper prepared by Philip Beisswenger during a student residence in Colombia (1982).

and Bolivian peasants, goes first to Colombia where it's refined into cocaine. Marijuana and counterfeit Qualuudes are also produced in quantity in Colombia's illegal drug labs.

Not entirely coincidently, murder is the leading cause of death in Colombia for persons between the ages of fifteen and forty-five. Bogota has the highest crime rate in the world.

Colombian violence goes far back in history, further than the current extremely profitable drug sales. The tendency toward murder is something we import along with Colombian drugs. It's one big reason why the drug scene can be so terrifying.

Colombian drug ringleaders in the United States are concentrated in Miami and New York City. Cocaine, processed in Colombia, is imported and distributed by a smooth-running, if lethal, organization.

There are also free-lance importers who go in planes and sailboats from the U.S. to Central America to buy cut-rate drugs.

Doug did this briefly.

Doug is illiterate. At the time he started school, his mother was abusing him so violently that he couldn't sit still. He certainly couldn't learn to read. Soon he didn't go to school anymore.

Instead of school, he picked up jobs in the building trades. It was easy to get him a job working on someone's house. Since he couldn't read, though, there was always some part of a job he couldn't handle. People felt justified in underpaying him.

Doug had had several convictions for petty theft. He would never steal from people he liked, but he never felt very bad about taking something from a warehouse.

Finally he decided to go west and see if he could get a better job. When he called us on Christmas Eve, he told us he was helping a man rebuild a sailboat. He proudly described the heavy brass instruments he had just installed.

Bob listened with interest to the details about the boat. We could both understand Doug's excitement at doing something interesting for a change, but I felt a little uneasy.

"Look, Doug," I heard Bob caution him, as they said goodbye. "Don't let anyone get you in trouble. Call us if you need us."

He hung up, then exploded. "First time in Doug's life anyone's treated him decently or given him a good deal—and it had to be a drug dealer!"

I wished Bob were wrong, but I knew he wasn't. We heard from Doug a couple of times after that, once from Mexico. Then there were several weeks of silence.

Finally, Doug called again. "They confiscated my boat!"

"What about you?" Bob asked. "Did you get confiscated?"

Doug had not been arrested. We never entirely understood the situation, but he was soon back in Nashville picking up poorly paid jobs where people were never very considerate.

I get angry about drug pushing but watching Doug made me understand it a little better. There are no rewards for Doug in our society. The only exception is that we keep the price of drugs high by keeping them illegal. Doug is agile and good at any mechanical task. I'm sure he loved maneuvering that sailboat around the Central American coastline. I wish I could think of something equally adventurous for him to do that is worth doing.

Drug use is certainly not new. There's archeological evidence that the coca plant, from which cocaine is derived, has been used for at least 5,000 years. Alcohol, peyote, and opium are samples of the mind-altering drugs that date back many centuries.

People have become afraid of heroin (one thing to be thankful for!) and sales are finally down. Largely produced in the Golden Crescent countries of Pakistan, Iran, and Afghanistan, heroin has been smuggled out through the Khyber Pass since ancient times.

Until 1906, when the Pure Food and Drug Act was passed, cocaine was treated casually in the United States. It was an ingredient in the original Coca Cola and in other soft drinks and patent medicines.*

The enormous profits from selling drugs tempt both the greedy and the desperate. Sheriffs and rich industrialists have

*From a series by Bill Snyder in the *Nashville Banner* August-September, 1983.

been arrested on charges of being involved in drug sales. I know young people who routinely sell a little marijuana if they're short on money to pay the electric bill.

Scott and a couple of his friends, also on drugs, stole his grandparents' family silver while his grandmother lay dying.

Barbara's son Harold broke into her house while he was drunk and on amphetamines. He left with everything in the medicine cabinet.

"Even the mouthwash!" Barbara said, exasperated. "And while he was at it, he also stole the TV and stereo—which he pawned."

Uppers like the amphetamines and cocaine also cause some violent crime. Downers like barbiturates, heroin, and Qualuudes are not apt to trigger aggressive activity. They make you sleepy.

What scares me most is the casualness with which some young people will drink or smoke anything that comes along.

Connie had started shooting up again and we were worried.

"How's she getting her stuff?" I asked one of her friends.

"Oh, she's got a scam. She can talk any man into anything, including a pharmacist, so she gets everyone's forged prescriptions filled. They pay off by giving her a cut."

"What's she on mostly?"

"Anything she can get her hands on—mixed."

It makes me remember back to first grade. We had a game, when grown-ups left us alone for a little while, in which we mixed "cocktails" for each other. Anything went—black pepper, shoe polish, cranberry juice, castor oil, whatever we could find that was reasonably liquid.

To save face, you had to drink the cocktail the other kids had mixed for you. If you could manage to feign enthusiasm, the others were really impressed. As far as I know, none of us had to have our stomachs pumped out, which was just amazing luck.

That was nearly a half century ago. Sometimes we sipped our cocktails while listening to "Little Orphan Annie" and "Jack Armstrong" on the radio.

Strange that kids today—big kids, teenagers or older—have

taken over our game. Except they use needles. We never would have. We were terrified of shots.

A kilogram of essentially pure cocaine cost about $50,000 in 1983. Mixed with grape sugar, coffee creamer, amphetamines, quinine, strychnine, or insect powders to stretch the supply, it rapidly becomes five kilograms of 20 percent strength cocaine. This is readily sold at $20,000 a pound, netting the dealer $170,000.*

"Why strychnine and insect powders?" I asked a friend who had had a lot of experience in the drug scene. "Won't those monsters stop at anything?"

He laughed. "I wouldn't say they worry about someone dying, but that's not the idea. Customers often test drugs before they buy them to see if they're contaminated. It's easy to test for coffee creamer and grape sugar so they spot fillers like that right away. Detecting strychnine and insect powders takes sophisticated equipment and most customers wouldn't know, anyway."

Both the Columbian drug dealers and the United States government prefer that drug prices stay high. The dealers are interested in profits, the U.S. government in discouraging customers, especially teenagers.

Late in 1983, good quality cocaine was sold in South Florida at $28,000 a kilogram. There are indications the price will continue to drop.** This will mean dealers have to sell more cocaine for the same income, and it will also mean that customers with less money can buy. So far, cocaine is still priced out of reach for most teenagers but experts are worried about lower prices putting cocaine into high schools. In 1982, the majority of Americans who had used cocaine were over twenty-six.

Cocaine shows up alongside the liquor at parties of entertainers and young professionals. Blue collar workers are even more likely to use it. It has an aura like the imported wine at an upper-class dinner during prohibition.

*Snyder, *Banner* series.
**Ibid

Breaking the law is part of the excitement for many users. It's cloak-and-dagger stuff, an adventure without doing anything they consider really *wrong*.

But cocaine is addictive. And it can seriously impair judgment, as well as have unpleasant physical effects, largely on the respiratory system. Its use by professionals scares some drug experts. What if your surgeon had a little cocaine to bolster his spirits for your difficult operation? Or a couple of Senators took a cocaine break while they were working on important legislation? This sort of thing *is* happening.

Organized crime lost interest in selling liquor at the end of prohibition. Liquor is still extremely profitable, but no longer *that* profitable. Ending prohibition obviously didn't reduce sales. Lately, sales of alcoholic beverages are down a bit as the result of the interest in physical fitness. That's the first slowdown since prohibition ended.

Looking at the lethal jungle surrounding drug sales, some experts recommend that we decriminalize some of the drugs. Most often, they recommend that marijuana be made legal in small amounts. Sometimes the plan is to sell it under rigidly controlled conditions as we do liquor. Other experts, just as concerned, oppose decriminalizing drugs. They predict that this would increase their use.

One knowledgeable campus minister said, "If you make marijuana legal, the kids will buy something stronger that isn't."

The National Academy of Sciences did not endorse the recommendation of its Committee on Substance Abuse and Habitual Behavior that possession or private use of small amounts of marijuana should no longer be a crime. The committee, although concerned about the long-range harm from marijuana use, was also concerned about the long-range harm of putting kids in jail.*

If we conclude that a drug is going to continue to be widely used whatever we do, it might make sense to have it available under tight restrictions. The price for marijuana could be too low

***Time Magazine* (July 19, 1982, p. 79).

to interest organized crime. It could be guaranteed free of rat poison, and bought in a regulated store where there's less danger of customers getting shot. Managing to regulate drugs so the drug merchants no longer can make obscene profits is certainly an appealing idea.

Some experts think drug use would eventually drop if new customers were not being constantly recruited by greedy drug dealers. Others think having drugs cheaper, more available, and safer would greatly increase their use. Lowering the legal age for buying alcohol did greatly increase its teenage use, including the younger friends of the eighteen or nineteen-year-old purchaser.

Eleven states, occupied by a third of the people in the United States, now use fines for marijuana use instead of arrests and incarceration.

Drug education is another area of controversy. People have enthusiastically tried classroom instruction about drugs, "rap houses" with former addicts as counselors, and innovative uses of TV, radio, pamphlets, and comic books.

There have been glowing reports about the success of some of the projects. There have also been hard questions from drug experts who feared that the main result was to make kids curious enough to experiment with drugs.*

I knew one drug counseling center which used young counselors who had served prison time for hard drug sales and use. They were excellent counselors, very helpful with a wide range of teenage problems. Later, though, at least one of the counselors went back to selling drugs, and one of the kids he'd worked with went with him.

My own worst experience has been with an anonymous paperback, *Go Ask Alice,* which high school guidance counselors sometimes use with teenage girls.** Alice, from a warm middle-class background, became heavily involved with drugs, ran away for a few months, and led an excitingly dangerous life, all detailed

---

*Interview with Agnes Sylte, R.N., of Vanderbilt Medical Center's drug and alcohol clinic.
**Anonymous *Go Ask Alice* (Englewood Cliffs, N.J.: Prentice-Hall, 1971).

in the book. In the end, she went home, went off drugs, and tried to put life back together. It didn't work. She was still killed by an overdose given her by druggie friends she has left behind.

I've seen half a dozen well-worn copies of *Go Ask Alice* in the jeans pockets of runaway girls on drugs.

◊ S E V E N ◊

Who can we afford to lock up?

One day we received a phone call from our bank officer. Someone was trying to cash a Project Return check which she thought was forged. I checked quickly and discovered that it was one of a whole sheet of checks that had been torn from the back of our checkbook. The checkbook is kept in our upstairs hideaway office where I do paper work. I began locking up more carefully.

The same man tried unsuccessfully to cash two more stolen checks. From the bank's description we recognized Matthew Wayne, who had come to our office once but had not kept his return appointment. His parole officer told us he had a growing stack of warrants for Matthew.

When I received my personal bank statement for the month, I found a forged check for $150 which the bank *had* cashed. I was startled by how convincingly my signature had been forged. Matthew must have stolen one of my personal checks out of my desk drawer along with the Project Return checks.

The bank refunded my $150, and our officer sent for the automatic camera's picture of the person who had cashed the check. When the picture came several days later, she phoned us to come identify it.

Bob and I hurried over.

Though the picture certainly looked familiar, it wasn't Matthew. Neither Bob nor I were quite sure enough to identify it on the spot.

Back in our office, Bob spoke first, "It sure looks like Sylvester, doesn't it?" he said, unhappily.

"That's what I thought but I didn't want to make a mistake. Isn't this his first week on that new job?"

Bob nodded glumly. Sylvester, a tall, dark, cheerful man in his late twenties, seemed perpetually in minor trouble. But he'd never done anything seriously wrong. He'd never had a job that paid more than minimum wage. We liked him, thought he showed some potential, and hoped we could help him get out of that revolving door to jail and workhouse and into a job with some future.

"His boss called to thank us for sending him," Bob said. "They really liked his work the first couple of days."

I felt confused. Unless Sylvester were more literate than I thought, he couldn't have done those skillful forgeries. It also seemed out of character for him to have invaded my upstairs office. But those bank pictures seemed clear evidence and I started getting angry. Apparently he'd really let us down.

"Somebody go get him," I said. "How about you, Harmon? Tell his boss Sylvester seems to be in trouble and we have to see him."

If Sylvester came, it would be voluntarily. We have no legal authority, and he's a physically powerful man. While I was waiting, I began to wonder if I should have sent two staff members. After the shock about the checks, I was braced for further trouble.

But Sylvester and Harmon soon walked in together, friendly as always. Sylvester wanted very much to see those bank pictures. He couldn't quite believe them. "And my good job," he added dismayed. "I've really blown it."

Harmon took him to the bank, and soon phoned me from the bank investigator's office. I went over to join them. It turned out that Matthew, finally realizing he wasn't having any luck cashing checks at our bank, had paid Sylvester $50 to cash the $150 forged check. It was stupid of Sylvester and certainly wrong, but it was hardly a major crime.

"And now I've got to fill out a bunch of forms and pay $12 for warrants," the investigator said, looking at Sylvester with distaste.

The story, plus Sylvester's obvious dismay, had gotten me over my anger. "What if I gave you $150 for the check?" I asked.

"If you give me $150, you can have the check *and* the man—and good riddance," the investigator said promptly.

"Let me see about a couple of things. I'll call you within an hour," I promised.

Harmon, Sylvester, and I went back to the Project Return office to do some homework.

A phone call to Sylvester's new employer solved most of the problems. He was willing to keep Sylvester on, and to hold his paycheck for the next three Friday afternoons. A Project Return staff member would meet Sylvester and they'd cash the check together. Then Sylvester would pay $50 each week toward his total debt of $150.

Since he'd only received $50 from the check, the $100 penalty seemed adequate punishment. Sylvester was enthusiastic about the idea, and almost tearfully grateful that his boss and Project Return had given him another chance.

The session of Downtown Presbyterian Church, which was meeting that night, agreed to loan us the $150.

Repayment went smoothly. We paid the bank, Sylvester paid us, we paid the session. The whole thing took a total of about six hours of staff time, and a few minutes of extra effort in the personnel office where Sylvester worked. If he'd gone back to prison, it would have been for at least six months, and would have cost taxpayers something over $6,000.

We also think Sylvester learned more from our simple solution. Two years later, he's still on the same job. There have been minor problems, but nothing we couldn't handle in the community.

Slightly over one out of every six hundred Americans is in prison. This figure does not include people in reform school or those in jail.

But for a couple of weeks longer, it does include Julia.

You would expect to see Julia taking a bouquet from her garden to an elderly, bargain hunting in the supermarket, pouring coffee for the missionary society—just about anywhere but prison.

She fatally shot her husband because he raped her twelve-year-old daughter, Laurie, his stepdaughter.

"The lawyer said if I'd caught him in the act and shot him then, no jury would have convicted me," Julia recalls in her soft voice. "I didn't, though—it took me three days to get that angry."

The first day had been taken up listening to Laurie's tearful story. Then they spent a half day in the hospital emergency room and talking to police.

Lying awake the next night, Julia could not stop thinking of the unbelievable things her husband had done to Laurie. Watching her child sobbing in the emergency room, Julia had thought she looked like one of those limp, furry squirrels her husband frequently brought home from hunting.

Julia knew where her husband kept his hunting rifle and she had watched him load it. Eventually she could think of nothing but getting out that rifle and going to find him.

One day at the woman's prison, Julia asked me about an educational release program. "I want to take licensed practical nursing," she explained eagerly. "I'd always planned to—just as soon as the kids were old enough."

Speaking of her children saddened her, as if someone had snuffed out a brightly burning candle. But the sadness lasted only a minute, and Julia went on with her eager questions. She was forty-two and attractive in a homey sort of way. Just the person you'd like to see if you were sick, I thought.

An assistant commissioner of the Department of Correction approved Julia's daytime release for the nursing course. Unfortunately, it didn't work out because of politics within the department. Soon he became the "wrong" assistant commissioner to give instructions to the wardens, and not long after, he resigned. Because departments of correction are usually intensely political, politics has a lot of effect on prisoners' daily lives.

Last week I had a nice note from Julia. She'd been paroled and would be going home in June. "I've finally applied for my nursing course," she added in a postscript.

During her six years in prison, Julia had mothered the younger girls, and helped some of them do constructive planning for the first time in their lives. Julia's sister and brother-in-law took care of Julia's children and brought them three hundred miles each month to visit her. For Julia, there will be life beyond prison.

Every women's prison includes some women a lot like Julia. Some had never stolen anything in their whole lives nor hurt anyone until the day they finally erupted into violence. The abuse to them or their children had become more than they could figure out how to handle except by assault or murder.

Certainly they should have found a better solution. But before we cast too many stones, let's remember how recently the rest of us have begun offering any help at all to women trapped in such brutal situations.

Anytime someone is killed or hurt, all of us have a problem to solve. But in a case like Julia's, is prison necessarily the best solution? Is the particular violence that triggered the crime likely to recur? Does it seem probable that Julia would hurt anyone else? Would you be worried if she moved next door to you, attended your church, or took a job in your office?

Would it be reasonable to work out a plan so that Julia, like Sylvester, could make restitution for her crime in the community, at the same time caring for and supporting her children?

Alternatives to prison are rarely designed for someone convicted of a crime like Julia's. They are far more likely to be used for minor crimes (misdemeanors), which are usually punished by spending time in a jail or workhouse. Typical misdemeanors include writing bad checks under $100, petty theft, possession of small amounts of illegal drugs, assault without a weapon, and public drunkenness.

Milton Rector, retired president of the National Council on Crime and Delinquency, warns against allowing alternatives to be used to "widen the net." We could easily find that by setting up good alternatives to prison, we were simply causing more people to be punished. The people might still be in prison who have always been in prison. But a lot of people who would have simply been set free, if we hadn't started our program, would be serving an alternative sentence instead.

When alternatives are used for serious crime (felonies), they are usually restricted to property crimes. While Julia's crime was violent, I think she'd be a good candidate for an alternative sentence. The firm line between violent and property crime isn't always valid.

Julia would be much easier to supervise in the community than a young career burglar, or a young man we know who has just finished a crime binge across fifteen states. His crimes were all technically property crimes, but there were a lot of them. He stole cars, motorcycles, credit cards, expensive jewelry, and high-priced electronic equipment.

In one northwestern town, he spent a night in a motel with a young woman. When she woke up, he was gone. So were her car, her diamond ring, and her billfold with nearly $1000. Although there's no bleeding victim to rush to the emergency room, that sort of crime certainly does violence to the human spirit.

The hardest problem in designing an alternative sentence for this young man would be figuring out how to keep track of him. If he chose, he could steal another vehicle and gasoline credit card, and be six states away very quickly.

The most urgent need for alternatives is for those which provide more effective supervision than the conventional state probation plans. Most people on probation report only once a month, and very briefly. Probation caseloads are enormous in most states, frequently something like three hundred people for each caseworker.

No matter how talented and concerned the probation officer is, with a caseload like that he or she is doing well to learn most of his clients' names. He certainly doesn't have time to build up a close relationship with many of them, or learn to recognize the signs of stress in each special person.

A crime often takes only about twenty minutes to commit, and is frequently triggered by alcohol or other drugs, general desperation, or a sudden specific crisis. Someone needs to be in close enough contact to know when Ted's wife has just left him, that he's in danger of losing his job, or that he's begun using too much alcohol or other drugs again. Many people commit crimes when their internal chemistry is out of kilter. Someone needs quickly to recognize depression, sudden irritability, or confusion. If Ted is already beginning to get in trouble, it is often possible to intervene right then to keep it from getting worse, *if* someone knows it right then.

Twenty probationers could be supervised by a skilled two-person team whom they meet with daily, at a total cost of about $2,000 a year for each person supervised. The cost of keeping those twenty people in prison would be about $30,000. (Both figures should be adjusted upward in states with high costs of living, but the ratio will be about the same.) Even more important than the huge savings to taxpayers, such a plan is considerably more likely to teach people how to function in the community. Restitution to victims should be part of each sentence whenever possible. Community service work can be substituted for restitution to the particular victim if necessary, and the whole group should plan to do occasional community service together. Programs like this can be structured so that the group itself becomes a powerful instrument for change.

One problem with designing occasional alternatives to prison is that most people *expect* people to go to prison when they commit crimes. The victim may feel that the crime is not being taken seriously, that the person who did the damage is getting off more lightly than most similar offenders.

Even more serious, the offender may feel that he is getting

preferential treatment. Jerry is an attractive young man who has for years been making his banker father frantic. Jerry's past crimes have been expunged after brief and interesting programs ordered by judges who were usually family friends. If Jerry were treated like most of the young people we work with, he'd be locked up somewhere and have a conviction record that fills a couple of index cards. He has confidence, though, based on a lot of experience, that this will never happen to him.

Many people who commit crimes feel that they can outsmart everyone else. They find it exciting to feel so powerful. It is dangerous to reinforce this viewpoint. An alternative sentence served in the community should include some tough changes in lifestyle, restitution to the victim, and community service. Most important, there should be continual supervision and follow-up. Such a sentence dare not be an empty gesture; it must be taken seriously and have teeth in it.

Con-wise is the term prisoners use to describe a standard con game played with rehabilitation people. At the time he (or she) is admitted to prison, the con-wise prisoner acts hostile, depressed, as unpromising as he can manage without being penalized with a longer sentence. Then he attaches himself to someone's pet pilot program, or an influential religious group that comes regularly to the prison. At first he's on the fringes, still distrustful, but gradually the delighted sponsors realize that they've changed a life. This formerly unpromising prisoner is one of their successes.

This particular story is surefire with parole boards, except for the occasional experienced parole person who automatically questions it. The hard-line questions horrify the sponsors of the program who are invariably there in behalf of this favorite prisoner.

Occasionally, a con-wise prisoner finds that he has received a larger reward than he ever dreamed of, and made a genuine commitment to the program he had intended to ride out of prison. Experienced observers can generally tell the difference, though. He talks less, does more.

These standard prison games will probably be played in programs in the community, too, and people who are working with community programs need to be aware of them. *Aware* need not mean cynical. Most of us know how to use gentle humor to handle a friend who is being manipulative. The same thing works with friends who have had criminal convictions.

One of the reasons that young people continue doing crime is that they realize how slim the chance is that they'll be caught.

Each law enforcement agency has jurisdiction limited to a small geographical area. By contrast, the people who commit crimes are frequently highly mobile.

Too frequently, people are never caught because it is too difficult to arrest and convict anyone who keeps crossing state lines. Although a lot of planning has been done on coordination and communications between police departments, it doesn't always work. If someone is arrested in New Jersey and can't be convicted without physical evidence which is in a police property room in California, his case will likely be dismissed.

Not always. If the crime was a murder, it is usually vigorously prosecuted. Rape and many armed robberies are also high priority crimes with most police departments. The FBI works effectively on federal cases as serious as bank robbery.

But when it comes to auto theft and burglaries under $100,000, police generally "make the cases" that don't require much effort in rounding up evidence. That's why so many incompetents, easily convicted of minor crimes, clutter our prisons, while people who continually commit serious felonies remain free.

I don't like prisons and I'm in favor of tough, carefully supervised community sentences for the majority of these young people. But they do need to be literally *arrested*—stopped. *Certainty* of punishment prevents crime far more than the length or severity of a sentence.

Not long ago in Richmond, a husband volunteered to serve his wife's jail term so she could care for their baby. I'm certainly in favor of the baby being cared for, but if I were a Virginia taxpayer, I would loudly protest this expensive Mickey Mouse game. If the community is safe with the wife home with her baby, fine. We certainly don't need to pay to keep someone else in jail to serve her sentence.

Now that we realize that prisons are a scarce and expensive resource, we need to pick with precision the people who must be locked up. If I had the authority to choose, I would use prisons only for people who are dangerous, or who cannot be deterred in a community program from continual burglary or car theft.

(Some people disagree about locking up career burglars and car thieves. They would never use prison for property offenses.)

There's an even more serious objection to prison sentences than cost to taxpayers. Serving a prison term is the rite of passage in becoming a criminal. Although they probably have done illegal things before, most people do not identify themselves as being outside the law until they are actually in prison. Then the convict's code, which they probably take very seriously, helps shape their future decisions and lifestyle.

There are people we should try especially hard never to lock up. Most important, some people in jail and prison are *innocent*. I used to be very skeptical when someone said, "I didn't do it," but experience is teaching me to listen more carefully.

Pedro, who has no family and grew up in foster homes and orphanages, was charged with a daylight burglary a few months ago. He was living in the suburbs and working in a restaurant at night. He told us he was home asleep when the burglary was said to have occurred about fifteen miles from his apartment. We believed him, but he couldn't prove it. And he was in jail when he told us.

A young man doing yard work next door to the burglary, said he had seen a "tall, blond guy" enter the house, and later leave it carrying something. The police showed the young yardman a book of mug shots. Sure enough, he picked out a picture of a tall blond—Pedro.

"Is that yard boy short and dark?" somebody at Project Return muttered, but no one took that seriously then.

Pedro, whose Nordic features are quite distinctive, was arrested and put in a lineup. The yardman identified him in the lineup also. Quite confident now that they had the right man, the police charged Pedro with burglary and had him held in jail. It was eight days before his girl friend could raise the $500 it took to make bond.

The restaurant where Pedro was working fired him because he'd been arrested.

The worst of his bad breaks was to be assigned to a judge who didn't get along with the public defender's office. Project Return talked to several lawyers whom we knew well and they all made the same suggestion—that Pedro get a young lawyer who had previously been a junior member of the judge's former law firm.

"He's the only person in town we can be sure Judge Harrington will listen to," one lawyer said grimly.

Since Pedro had lost his job, some of our other lawyer friends would have handled his case for free, or a very small fee. It would have been free if handled by the excellent public defender's office. But the lawyer he needed, because of the politics involved, was just setting up practice, and said he'd have to charge $1000. Pedro had a $400 income tax return coming back eventually, and some of his friends put together $200 as a down payment on the lawyer's fee. The other $400 he'd have to manage to pay somehow.

His lawyer suggested that Pedro volunteer to take a lie detector test. He did—in fact he eventually took two, and passed them both. These were a big help in court, but they cost Pedro another $60.

By the time the charges were finally dropped, nearly three months later, Pedro's legal expenses had gone over $1800. After losing his job, he had picked up some daywork, but his income was so drastically reduced that he was nearly evicted from his apartment.

After he was cleared, the restaurant where he had worked rehired him.

"I guess in a couple of years, I'll get out of this hole," Pedro said. "Unless something else comes up. The detective says they *are* questioning the yardboy about the burglary. Turns out he's a high school kid, dark and not very tall."

The first time I heard about an illiterate being locked up for writing a bad check, I thought it was a joke. Unfortunately, it wasn't. It happens frequently. Casey didn't write a check. He just endorsed his name to a bad check someone had given him for some work. His name is the only thing Casey *can* write, and it's pretty hard to read. He got a workhouse sentence.

Daryl, who had gone through school in a learning disabilities class, stole a checkbook from his church. It was in the desk at home; his father was church treasurer.

He wrote some checks and tried to cash one at the bank. The bank didn't cash it—no danger of anyone cashing a check Daryl wrote!—but they did have him arrested for "uttering a forged instrument." He spent a couple of days in jail, and was found guilty at trial. Fortunately, he was given probation.

His father and his minister are trying to explain the ethics of the situation to him. I hope they succeed. They are certainly better qualified than the criminal justice system.

George Whittaker is fascinated by banks and writes bad checks all the time. Although he is in his twenties, he really couldn't handle first-grade schoolwork. It's hard to believe anyone would cash a check George wrote, but occasionally someone does. Mainly the checks just make him feel important, although he enjoys money when he does get some. His check writing is a lot like playing with play money.

It was very real money, though, that we taxpayers paid for George's two prison terms for writing bad checks.

California has quit using criminal penalties for crimes involving checks and other paper transactions. People can sue in civil court to recover losses.

"You'd be surprised how much more careful they've gotten out there about cashing checks in a bar for a drunk," Harold Bradley, formerly Tennessee Commissioner of Correction, commented.

I have a lot of confidence in businesses and banks. I believe they can manage to coexist with George without either losing much money, or finding it necessary to have him locked up.

Big reasons for hesitating to lock someone up are the prisoner's health and safety. All of us read with horror about a 17-year-old Idaho boy who was tortured to death by five other 17-year-olds in a jail cell. The boy's crime? He owed sixty dollars worth of unpaid traffic tickets.

Jail fires are notorious and lethal. Besides concern for the welfare of the juvenile, a strong reason for never holding juveniles in adult jails is the chance of their starting fires. A lot of delinquents have been starting fires since they were preschoolers. Setting something on fire is a frequent act of defiance for a youngster who finds himself locked up, and the majority of jails are firetraps.

Even the brand-new jails with computer-operated gates worry prisoners, possibly with good reason.

"The computer is down a lot," one of them told me. "We were all locked in the dining room for ten minutes while they were trying to get it fixed. What would happen if there were a fire while it was down?"

Prisoners frequently kill themselves, a good indicator of the pain and humiliation of being locked up. Even when the lockup is an attempt at solving a serious problem, we should look at other possible solutions.

We must keep drunks off our roads. Someone who's been convicted once of DUI (driving under the influence) is a lot more likely to kill us than someone who's been convicted once of murder.

But we can probably think of more effective ways to do that than putting them in jail. Locking up the car would be a great deal cheaper, more humane, and probably more effective. If someone unwisely loaned or rented a car to a person whose own car was impounded for DUI, that car should also be impounded. If necessary, a car could be kept locked up for months, or even auctioned off to cover damage done, if the state enacted appropriate legislation.

Sometimes temporary lockup prevents assault or murder, or stops an unstable person from continuing a series of crimes. Before we tell police that they may not use a jail for these purposes, we need to have something else to offer. We should work on some creative alternatives to holding people in jail.

A jail is supposed to be a place to hold people who have not been convicted of anything. It should be designed for emergency use, somewhat analogous to a hospital emergency room. Single cells are imperative since there's no time for classifying prisoners. Besides the possibilities of murder, rape, and fights, infections spread rapidly in crowded jail cells.

A responsible community should see to it that its jail is a place where anyone's son or daughter could be held overnight without danger of permanent harm. If you think families like yours are in no danger of having a young person in jail, you'd better read the morning paper carefully.

The community jail should be as harmless as we can make it and used as little as we can arrange.

The recent arrests for computer crimes remind us that it's more effective to prevent a crime than to punish the offender afterwards. Theft by computer should be punished like any other grand larceny, but the invasions of data banks by bright computer kids can surely be handled differently. I would consider sentencing some of them to help design a foolproof system of keeping people from altering data, and preferably, a foolproof system of keeping people from calling up data. The problem can be solved, like many others, if we don't get sidetracked into using up all our ingenuity on punishment instead.

Long prison terms often result in broken health. If a young prisoner already has a chronic disease when he or she enters prison, this is almost certain to become more serious.

We're concerned about two young men right now. One has worked on the Project Return staff. The other is a favorite volunteer. Both are in their mid-twenties, served about five years for armed robbery, and have juvenile type diabetes. In spite of all the coincidences, they didn't know each other until they met in our office. They've been in and out of hospitals all year, have both had laser surgery on their eyes, and before the year is over, both will either have to need kidney transplants or have to go on dialysis.

Harold, a man assigned to Project Return on work release, had such high blood pressure that it caused retinal hemorrhages, and the doctor was worried about a heart attack or stroke. Harold flatly refused to go to the hospital, which would have meant being behind the walls of the main prison. A sympathetic doctor agreed to care for him as an outpatient, and managed to get his blood pressure down to a safer reading. To everyone's relief, his eventual release from prison caused it to drop nearly to normal.

The physical stress of being a prisoner can be very long-term punishment.

Changes in criminal justice that will affect thousands of people's lives will be those made by governments. The role of small agencies like Project Return, and the dozens of others spotted around the United States and Canada, is to try new ideas, stimulate discussion, and establish pilot programs. Our small size and flexibility are a strength when it comes to being innovative.

An agency exists as a tool for a group of churches or other sponsors to use for work they consider important. It's important that we remember there are other ways for a church to work. An adult Sunday school class can sponsor a person coming out of prison and building a new life in the community. Some space in a church basement and a few volunteers committed to reconciliation have often created miracles in lives that desperately need miracles. This continues to work, and is exactly the way most of the existing agencies began.

These are not innovative, far-out ideas for Christians. They are just a simple, daily application of the gospel—things Christians have been doing since the days when Paul was writing letters to churches.

We are commanded to be the leaven that can start dramatic changes in the whole loaf.

We can work at replacing polarized court fights with negotiation by setting up dispute centers to handle civil and criminal cases. (Probably minor ones in the early stages.)

We can use all our creativity in handling human problems in human sorts of ways, with the victim our focus of concern.

One leader in prison reform said: "You can nearly always work out an alternative to prison if it's for your child."

And if it's for a child of God?

◊ E I G H T ◊

Loving, responsible killing?

On Friday, April 22, 1983, Alabama went back into the capital punishment business after 16 years without killing anyone. One of her sons, John Evans, dropped his appeals and threw himself on the mercy of Governor George Wallace. Wallace promptly ordered him electrocuted.

When Thomas A. Edison invented the electric chair, it was touted as instantaneous and painless. Evans didn't die instantly and he didn't die painlessly. Although nobody knows how long he remained conscious, the doctors found his heart still beating after both the first and second charges of electricity. It took a third charge of electricity to finally kill him.

Evans himself had killed someone. Almost the only way you can get to death row, since the Supreme Court required the states to rewrite their capital punishment laws, is by having a jury convinced that you killed someone.

A life for a life? Possibly. If killing Evans could have restored his victim to life, I'd feel like taking a long, fresh look at the whole question.

But in this real world, it sounds a good deal more like *two* people murdered.

When I was a small child, they killed a lot of people—I guess partly for me. Born in 1929, I grew up in the 1930s when executions were commonplace. In 1933, the worst year on record, four people a week were judicially murdered in the United States.

I don't think I ever *favored* the death penalty, but as a child (and even in college) I certainly didn't think about it much.

It was years later before I read the protests of the corrections people who were stuck with doing society's killing in the 1930s—and during the worst period of unemployment this nation has ever known. A man with a family might have had to think hard before he'd sacrifice the only job in sight, no matter how distasteful.

Clinton T. Duffy, formerly warden at San Quentin who participated in 150 executions, said that 90 percent of the prison wardens in the United States opposed the death penalty.*

They were in the informed minority in the 1930s. In 1936, 62 percent of Americans favored the death penalty.

Lewis Lawes, formerly warden at Sing Sing, used to invite judges and prosecutors to view the executions they had ordered. None ever accepted.

However, hundreds of other people did beg Lawes to allow them to watch executions. When a new executioner was to be hired, Lawes was appalled by the hordes of eager applicants, some willing to kill for cut-rate wages.

Corrections people sometimes voiced suspicion that we were killing an occasional innocent person in our rush to the electric chair. The convictions of black men for raping white women seemed especially apt to be in error, considering the passions of the time. No white man was ever executed for raping a black woman, although white men did indeed rape black women.

These were things I first learned in the 1950s in the civil rights movement. Friends I met then insisted that I also think about the death penalty.

It seems so impossible to me now that a sensitive, ethical person could favor executing people that I think it's important to remember how slowly my own ideas evolved.

*Clinton T. Duffy, *88 Men and 2 Women* (New York: Doubleday, 1963).

It is easy for any of us to become self-righteous about convictions that now seem self-evident. Putting forth the effort it takes to remember the painful learning processes *we* went through makes it possible to be more helpful to others now facing those same difficult decisions.

Even in the 1950s, I'm afraid my opposition to the death penalty was largely from self-interest. I didn't want the state to kill people for *me*.

I can remember saying, "I don't have any hopes about the salvage value of anyone who's made it to death row."

Back then, I'd never met anyone who'd made it to death row. I'd also never taken a good look at the gospel, the good news that is more relevant on death row than anywhere else on earth.

I probably *had* read the Old Testament story about a man who made a comeback after a particularly distasteful murder and was allowed to continue to do special service for God. Psalm 51 is believed to have been written by David as he contemplated the disasters he had created by his conspiracy to murder Bathsheba's husband, and asked for guidance for a better future.

But like a lot of people, I didn't expect biblical ideas to have anything to do with the real world. Not really. Although we talk a lot in houses of worship about people's potential for change, that change seems incredible the first time you really see it.

In 1966, the majority of Americans opposed the death penalty. Only 42 percent were in favor, the lowest support for capital punishment on record in the United States.

In 1967, the federal courts suspended all executions in the United States while the U.S. Supreme Court prepared itself to rule on whether the death penalty was "cruel and unusual punishment."

During that period, I went one Sunday to Calvary Presbyterian Church at Big Lick, Tennessee, to cover a news story. The pastor of the small country church uphill from Crossville had just been elected moderator of the United Presbyterian Church in its national convention at Portland, Oregon.

Doing background research later for my story, I discovered that Dr. Eugene Smathers, the pastor, was well known to theologians and had been doing pioneer work in health care and community organizing about the time I was learning to talk. As moderator, he chose the first black vice-moderator in the history of the United Presbyterian Church.

But before the Sunday he returned from Portland and gave a report to the home folks, I'd never heard of either Dr. Smathers or his church. My experience with churches and with Christians had been mostly negative, and this slim crew-cut six-footer and his community impressed me a lot.

The church building, pretty and nostalgic, is surrounded by big evergreens. From the churchyard, one can view some of the loftiest peaks in the Cumberlands. The congregation built it themselves, partly of local Crab Orchard stone, in 1935. It's the only church I've ever encountered built in that depression year.

"We were all out of work and figured we ought to do something good with our spare time," one old man explained.

Later, whenever my life got hectic, I'd promise myself that one day I'd go back up to Big Lick for a Sunday service.

Then, while Dr. Smathers was still moderator, there was a murder at Big Lick. Two parolees from Indiana, who had been drinking continuously for several days, had pursued a 20-year-old man into someone's house and shot him nine times.

Other young men, lifelong friends of the victim, stormed the jail and the two murderers had to be moved to another county for safekeeping.

Other unusual touches were reported. At their trial, one of the two defendants sat taking notes.

Unlike the close-knit community at Big Lick, I hadn't known the young victim. My feeling was that something I valued had been violated. I watched the trial closely, and each detail shocked me. Big Lick just seemed the most unlikely place on the planet for a murder.

Because of the suspension on executions, the jury feared that giving the two defendants the death penalty might somehow result in their being freed. Instead, they sentenced each man to 318 years in prison.

In 1972, the Supreme Court declared all existing death penalty laws unconstitutional. Legislators in several states promptly got busy drafting new laws that they hoped would be acceptable.

In 1976, the Supreme Court ruled North Carolina's new law that made death mandatory for first degree murder unconstitutional. Louisiana's similar law was also rejected. At the same time, the Court also ruled that the death penalty was not inevitably unconstitutional by approving the laws just passed by Georgia, Texas, and Florida.

Late in 1975, I had moved to Nashville and gone back to college, after spending a quarter-century raising a houseful of boys.

I soon found that some of my classmates were prisoners, and several became my friends. One was Rich, who always came to a Saturday group dynamics class with a buddy none of us realized was his guard.

The natural leader of the group, bright, sensitive, and rumored to have a straight A average, Rich impressed all of us.

We were mildly surprised when we realized, from some of his comments in class, that he was serving time for a violent crime.

Then one day, someone asked Rich when he'd be eligible for parole.

He laughed. "With good time, maybe a little before 2100. I've served nine years of a 318-year sentence."

I gripped the arm of my chair hard, suddenly feeling sick and dizzy. I knew of only two men in Tennessee serving 318 years. But how could someone like Rich, someone I *liked,* have possibly killed the boy at Big Lick?

He wondered, too, I discovered later. His bright, perceptive teenage daughters came to visit. A grandmother was doing a great job of raising them under conditions which were bound to be difficult.

As the older daughter's 20th birthday approached, Rich was

increasingly haunted by remembering the boy he had killed.

"If it would make his family feel any better, I'd lie down on their front porch and shoot myself," he said, "but it's hard to believe it would help. I wish there were something I could do for them without them knowing who did it."

In 1977 the death penalty came back. Five men in Utah fired guns at Gary Gilmore. One gun was loaded with a blank, which was supposed to leave some lingering hope with each member of the firing squad that he hadn't really been the one to do the killing.

It was actually an expensive and obscenely publicized suicide. Gilmore wanted to die but apparently considered facing a firing squad more macho than just taking an overdose or turning on the gas.

The strongest argument the people who favor the death penalty like to use is that it deters violent crime. Only two out of forty-three studies of the death penalty claim to have found a clear deterrent effect.

Gilmore's case shone a disconcerting light on another possibility: that violent and unstable people actually commit murder in order to be executed.

George F. Solomon, M.D., wrote in the July 1975, *Journal of Osthopsychiatry* about a young woman, 20, who murdered two preschool girls she was baby-sitting.

She was fond of the children, she explained to police, and she knew their mother valued them, but she had tried suicide so many times without success that she had chosen an especially horrible murder, confident that the state would then end her life which she felt such a burden.

There also seem to be people who are simply incited to violence by reported violence. One California study showed a little ripple of violence following each legal execution. And a study of all executions in New York state between 1907 and 1963 showed an average of two additional homicides the month after every execution.

Assassins, especially, seem to be screaming for someone finally to notice them, whatever the price.

Commenting on Gary Gilmore's worldwide notoriety as a result of his death sentence, Norman Mailer said, "Unknown six months ago, one more con with half his life in jail . . . by this [execution] night in January, he has become one of the best-known faces in the world. *Time Magazine*, in its roundup at the end of the year, put his picture on the same two pages with Jimmy Carter and Rosalyn and Miz Lillian, put it there with Betty Ford and Mao Tse-tung and Henry Kissinger. What a deterrent!"

I'd had some experience with juvenile corrections, and now was deeply concerned about the futures of my prisoner fellow students. It was one of them who suggested that I do my graduate school internship in a little CETA-funded agency that was trying to find jobs for people leaving prison.

When that agency folded promptly (as federally funded projects have a way of doing), we started our own—Project Return. Among our friends and board members were the people at Southern Prison Ministry and Tennesseans Against the Death Penalty.

As 1979 got underway, the people involved in death row ministry became more and more worried about a friend on Florida's death row, John Spenkelink, who had nearly exhausted his appeals.

I never met John but I learned from many worried conversations how he looked, how he talked. I saw letters he wrote. And I watched the frantic attempts of young men who had become his close friends to keep him from being intentionally killed.

"Wasted" is the word. I understood for the first time how Vietnam veterans use it.

I have had friends who were terminally ill, even a baby who was facing death, and I know that desperation to somehow push away the threat which keeps coming closer.

This was worse. It was intentional. The legal maneuvers were like a chess game but John's life was the stake. And the opponent was a nearby state in these United States.

John Spenkelink wrote a letter to Governor Robert Graham whose job it would be to decide whether to sign John's death warrant. He suggested that Graham might want to take a look at him before ordering him killed. Graham didn't.

The governor of Florida is paid $59,098 a year (with fringe benefits like the executive mansion). It is assumed that he is an extraordinary man with extraordinary talents. His job gives him a lot of options about how he spends his time.

Graham has chosen to spend a lot more time signing death warrants (45 by January 1983) than he has in meeting the human beings whose deaths he is ordering.

But after John Spenkelink had already been killed in Florida's electric chair on May 25, 1979, Graham ordered an inquiry. He was upset by reports that guards had handled John brutally while getting him ready to die.

Florida prison guards are paid a small fraction of the governor's salary. Every payday most of them face a stack of bills to pay if their kids are to have shoes and a roof over their heads.

Choices are a luxury most guards figure they can't afford. If one of them had objected to helping kill John Spenkelink, he probably would have expected to find himself unemployed, with explanations to make to his cold and hungry family.

Riding toward their jobs at the penitentiary, the guards, like almost everyone else in the area, listened to the Greaseman on their car radios. The Greaseman, a local disc jockey, used frying bacon sound effects to show John Spenkelink how he'd sound when the state of Florida fried him in its electric chair.

Anyone who objected to this barbaric use of the public's airwaves didn't protest effectively enough to stop it.

During basic training, Marine recruits are taught to chant "Kill, kill, kill" while lunging bayonets into training dummies. Similarly, the people of Florida, and especially the guards who would have to actually do the job, were psyching themselves up to kill John Spenkelink.

Spenkelink was a man a lot of friends could love. But assuming you had wanted him dead, how would you have felt about the process of killing him? Would you have been willing to give people the message that human life isn't worth much, and the likes of the Greaseman are okay guys?

How would you have felt about the elaborate precautions against suicide after Graham had signed John Spenkelink's death warrant? His mother as subjected to a humiliating strip search before each visit, so they could be sure she was not smuggling in some painless lethal dose. Even John's pastor had trouble taking him communion. The officials feared a compassionate poison in the bread and wine.

Would you have been willing personally to pull the switch? If not, who would you have chosen to do the job for you? Is this someone you'd want living next door? If we consider executing people a public service, why do we keep the executioner's name such a top secret?

In an article about Tennessee's death row, Joseph Sweat pointed out some facts of life: "When the executioner is about to throw the switch, he protects himself by wiggling his hand into a rubber electrician's glove. It is heavy and black and reaches halfway to his elbow. Your hand is in that glove. He is doing this for you."*

If we had been present when the crime occurred—when the old lady was robbed at gunpoint, when the child was abused, when the car was stolen and its owner shot—we would have certainly tried to prevent it. If there were no other possible way to save the victim, most of us would have resorted to violence.

Whether we *should* have resorted to violence is another question. Dave Jackson has pointed out in *Dial 911: Peaceful Christians and Urban Violence* (Herald Press, 1981) that Jesus did not command us to turn our *neighbor's* cheek.

But the death penalty is violence that does nothing for the victim. The person to be killed is already in secure custody. Killing him is a public, dramatic act of revenge.

---

*Joseph Sweat, "Anatomy of an Execution" *Nashville Magazine* September, 1979, p. 42.

I don't want to kill people. I don't want *anyone* to kill people, especially not in *my* name, to express *my* vengeance.

A murder horrifies me but I can dimly understand it when it results from a fight, when a romantic triangle rouses ancient passions, when there's the lethal combination of alcohol and a gun. But planning to put cyanide in the neighbors' milk bottles, or making a businesslike contract to kill off an inconvenient person for pay—what kind of monster can do things like that?

And what kind of monsters do we expect to shave a man's head, forcibly strap him into a death chair, watch his face while they fasten electrodes to his head and calves, and turn on the high voltage (with a brief pause for a prayer designed to make everyone present, presumably including God, feel better).

Or to use medical expertise, life-*saving* expertise, to inject death into a human being's veins?

There *are* people on this planet who can intentionally kill people and even enjoy it, but we try to keep them confined to the locked wards of mental hospitals. Some people have found them useful. Without their enthusiastic help, Hitler could never have killed six million Jews plus a lot of the most decent Christians in Europe.

Even columnist William F. Buckley, an outspoken advocate of the death penalty, wrote a piece protesting Spenkelink's execution. There were aspects of self-defense about the killing that Spenkelink had committed. It simply didn't seem the horrifying kind of crime for which the death penalty is presumably reserved.

Unfortunately, Buckley's column ran after Spenkelink was already dead.

A judge can reverse an opinion or a higher court can; an innocent person can be released from prison is we discover that the conviction was a mistake. But whatever evidence and opinions we discover after we've killed someone can make no difference.

There are a number of well-documented cases of someone being killed for a crime which it was proved, *after they were dead,* that they didn't commit. There are also frequent close escapes.

For example, legal questions about the death penalty fortunately postponed the executions of six death row prisoners in Florida and New Mexico. In Florida, two black men, Freddie Pitts and Wilbert Lee, were released from prison in 1975 after 12 years awaiting execution for a murder someone else was found to have committed.

Only a few months later, New Mexico released four death row prisoners who had served eighteen months under identical circumstances.

In 1980, Georgia released two death row prisoners whose sentences had been overturned. One of them, Jerry Banks, who had maintained throughout six years on death row that he was innocent, never recovered. Just three months after his release, he and his wife were both found dead, an apparent murder-suicide.

A great many people who have served time on death row are later released to the general prison population by a judge or governor who decides that, although they are guilt, they are not *that* guilty.

Several times a state has found out for sure that someone already executed was innocent. It gives you a shaky feeling that maybe we'd better postpone making life-and-death decisions until we learn how to give someone's life back.

People sometimes say death is no worse punishment than a long prison term. Certainly human life is finite enough so it is painfully wasteful to have the years ticked off behind bars. But a person alive and in prison has possibilities—including, of course, the possibility of being freed and receiving some attempt at restitution, if we should someday discover he's been locked up in error.

Since he was nine years old, Ron Harries has been in prison almost continuously. Now 32, he used some of his abundant free time as an inmate on Tennessee's death row to add up all the scraps of time he'd spent in the free world. In the past 23 years, they totaled only 26 months.

Although Ron doesn't try to excuse the previous crimes, he does say that the murder which brought him to death row was actually an accidental shooting. However, his main interest now is to invest his own painful experience in something he considers worth doing—helping kids handle difficult lives more successfully than Ron himself has.

With another death row inmate, he interested the Nashville Southwest YMCA outreach director in the idea of "Starting Point," a program for boys who appeared headed for serious trouble. For four weekly sessions, they were brought to death row to be counseled by death row prisoners.

The first session with the original four boys chosen for the program was a disappointment to Ron. Since he himself had grown up, he had never spent time with teenagers. If he had, he would probably have guessed that these four were being cocky, and even rude, because they were scared.

"We certainly didn't have any 'Scared Straight' scam in mind," Ron explained. "We did want to relate to the kids as human beings who cared about them. We knew they needed to look at reality, and we'd figured we could get their attention just because of where we've wound up.

"That first day, though, we weren't so sure anymore."

By the next week, things looked more promising. The boys quit trying to impress death row inmates by acting cool and tough, and were visibly pleased at the concern shown. "We care about you and we want you to wind up better than we did" is a powerful message.

The program also made a strong impression on some of the boys' parents and guardians. They were startled that their youngsters had been selected for such a program and suddenly seemed to take parenting more seriously.

By the end of the four-week program, all four boys looked better groomed and were pleasanter to talk to. One had gone back to school and two had found jobs. Ron and his buddy were elated. They had not had too many chances in their lives to help people in important ways.

It takes ingenuity and a little luck to be able to make a contribution from a five-by-eight death row cell. There are a lot of long-termers in prisons, though, who were on death row until a successful appeal, or who narrowly missed a death sentence for a capital crime.

Most of them have painful regrets about the youthful crimes which landed them here, and regrets about the limits of their restricted lives. Many of them make valuable contributions.

There's Rich who finished three years of college with straight A's, and is now teaching illiterates to read in one of the regional prisons. He's president of the Alcoholics Anonymous group and uses his limited spare time to work on a novel. With his 318-year sentence, his only hope for eventual freedom is clemency granted by some governor sometime, and that may be a pretty slim hope. Rich's life, although certainly limited and wistful, is still definitely worth living.

Larry lived on death row for nearly two years until his conviction was reduced by the appeals court. Now 25, he organized the Parents in Prison program at Tennessee State Prison which gives inmates training in parenting and successful family life.

Two of the best staff members we've had at Project Return had served long sentences (which earlier could have been death), one for a murder during an armed robbery, one for rape.

Both men have become totally different people from the ones who committed the crimes, yet they both appear a little haunted by the memory of hurting someone. It is possible for crime and prison, like any other tough experience, to make someone responsible and perceptive. With these men, it did.

One of them, Allen, was talking to men still in Tennessee State Prison when Project Return put on a program there.

They listened intently as he told them how tough it could be to reenter the world outside, but how satisfying and challenging.

"All of us here have already learned how low we can go," he said, speaking softly. "Now we have a real chance—a chance to learn how high we can go."

The Christian story isn't about God helping good people become a trifle better. The Creator who tosses hundreds of thousands of galaxies around was perfectly capable of turning Nathan Leopold, a rich, spoiled thrill killer who barely escaped execution, into an outstandingly altruistic man. *And* it happened in prison, always the least likely seeming place in the world for a miracle.

Both my faith and my job have taught me never to give up on a person.

Nevertheless, most of us could name a grim list of people who we *never* want walking among us again. Gacy, Manson, Speck—I don't want to suddenly encounter any of those, or others who seem similarly dangerous, walking free.

That's what some people who favor the death penalty are thinking about. One of them told me, "It'll sure deter *that* guy from hurting anyone else."

But there *was* Leopold. Suppose there is a big, dramatic change over a period of years which is obvious to everyone? A jury found the person guilty in an open courtroom. Possibly a similar jury should find him rehabilitated and ready for release (under, I would think, pretty tight probation). The open courtroom would need to be part of the story. This is a decision made by and for all of us.

I think we should explore more possibilities for "forever" sentences in rare and dangerous situations. Some states have them in some form or other. We could call them something like the Mandatory Maximum with no parole, and expect prison authorities to see that the rare person so classified is no threat to other people locked up with him.

In most states, parole board hearings are public, and the judges and prosecutors who convicted the prisoner have a specific chance to protest or even advocate his/her release. Anyone else may be present to testify, too, but the general public is rarely aware of this.

You can feel quite strongly about the death penalty as a moral question when you aren't acquainted personally with any of the people affected. After meeting families, and individuals who have barely escaped death row, it becomes a human problem. You feel a lot more strongly.

But to really understand the death penalty and its horror, you need actually to go to death row and meet the men who literally live in the shadow of death.

They are our brothers, our sons, our fathers, our neighbors—speaking theologically. But most of them are related to us in everyday ways, too. They're human. Attractive, or not so attractive. Like people we live with, work with, love.

If you show that you feel a little overwhelmed by seeing a man squeezed into a five-by-eight cell, together with everything he has left in this world, you might get kidded a little.

"It *would* be a pretty small bathroom, but it's really quite large if you consider it a rabbit hutch."

Or if you're really accepted, someone might tell you about a new warden who came back to death row to meet the inmates.

He had just been promoted from head of a boys' reform school and was proud of his new status—partly, probably because he was about the size of Napoleon.

"I'm the man who'll pull the switch," he said, by way of introducing himself.

One considerably taller inmate craned his neck way back to get a better look at the pint-sized warden. After a careful scrutiny, he slowly shook his head.

"That so, sonny?" he asked gently. " 'Fraid you're going to have to stand on a ladder."

Once you've sentenced a man to death, you've lost most of your power over him.

All my swirling thoughts about the death penalty were focused for me by an unlikely seeming person: Carl Koella, the legislator who wrote Tennessee's new death penalty law after the Supreme Court had declared all existing laws unconstitutional.

Koella, obviously a thoughtful person as well as a skillful politician, explained why he thought the death penalty necessary: the strong feelings of his constituents, deterrent value, the necessity for a strong reaction to a particularly heinous crime, and all the rest.

Then, softly, he added something that he had obviously thought about a good deal. "But it *isn't* Christian."

Texas attorney Daniel H. Benson, who also teaches law, agrees. "One either follows the command to love even one's enemies, and in that case does not kill those enemies. Or one resolutely kills one's enemies as needed from time to time. In that event, of course, one does not and cannot love them."

◊ NINE ◊

"I was in prison . . ."

Most Christians who are interested in criminal justice issues are intensely conscious of Jesus' instructions to "seek and save that which was lost": lost sheep, lost coins, prodigal sons.

Other Christians join many Mennonites, Quakers, Brethren, and the National Council on Crime and Delinquency in opposition to building more prisons. They think most people convicted of wrongdoing should be dealt with in the community, and oppose capital punishment as "judicial murder."

It is hard to realize that there are Christians who take their faith seriously and yet view wrongdoers very differently. They even give biblical justification for their views sometimes, views which sound more like a "search and destroy" mission.

Why so much ambiguity? What does the Bible actually teach about crime, victims, forgiveness, and reconciliation?

To find God's words on crime, on evildoing, we don't need to *search* the Scriptures. Even when we open the Bible at random, they blaze out at us from practically every page. God's words: steadfast love, justice, reconciliation, kindness, peace, repentance, faith, hope, redemption, new life, being born again, grace, and forgiveness seventy-times-seven times.

Paul was welcomed into the Christian community (a little cautiously) with Christian blood on his hands but the Damascus Road drama in his heart. Jacob, despite business dealings that would have alarmed the Better Business Bureau, wrestled with God and fathered Israel's twelve tribes, God's chosen people.

Moses and David both did monumental work for God, even after each had committed, and been forgiven for, murder. (In Moses' case, extenuating circumstances would probably have reduced the charge to manslaughter. David's conspiracy to kill Bathsheba's husband, however, would be first-degree murder in most courts.) Jesus ate with tax collectors, sinners, and women who had been, to say the least, indiscreet. New life is an accomplished fact, a gift free for the taking.

Since the thirty-nine books of the Old Testament cover events over 2,000 years (much longer if we estimate a time span for the primeval events in the first eleven chapters of Genesis) and were actually written over a 700-year period (roughly 900-200 B.C.), they naturally reflect a great deal of change in the way people understand God's law.

By contrast, all 27 New Testament books were written in less than a century, all around the central theme of Jesus' life, death, and teachings, and in response to specific needs of the early Christian churches. Understandably, when we start examining a subject as broad as crime and punishment, we find more consistency of viewpoint in the tighter timespan of the New Testament.

However, throughout the entire Bible, we find an important thread of grace. Jesus, raised a Jew, "earnestly desired" to celebrate the traditional Passover feast with his disciples on the evening he was to be arrested and soon crucified (Luke 22:15). He was heir not only to the bloodlines of Abraham and David, but to the teachings of the prophets about mercy and righteousness. All his life, he quoted from the Old Testament, which he knew intimately. In the agony of the worst moment of his human life, his spontaneous outcry was a quotation from Psalm 22: "My God, my God, why hast thou forsaken me?" (Mark 15:34).

Even in the oldest books of the New Testament, the five books of the law (Genesis—Deuteronomy) and Joshua, we still find passages that shine for us today. They are imbedded in an intricate and fascinating network of laws, public health ordinances, and detailed religious ritual—the commandments which transformed a nomadic tribe, surrounded by fertility cults, idols, and bloody ideas of wholesale revenge, into God's chosen people.

Today, nearly 3,500 years after Moses, not only the Ten Commandments but many of the other legal concepts still have a powerful influence on the laws under which we live. But not enough influence. Our criminal justice code is more influenced by Roman law than by Judeo-Christian teachings.

From earliest times, Jewish law gave special protection to the poor, the widow, the orphan. For a wide variety of sins and crimes, the usual consequences were atonement to God with specified sacrifices, restitution to neighbor, or death (most often by stoning).

Even the laws which sound cruel were usually a constraint on what had been normal practice earlier. "An eye for an eye and a tooth for a tooth" (Exodus 21:24), for example, substituted limited revenge and a legal system, for the previous rampant revenge in which you murdered anyone who had wronged you, along with his kinfolk, and probably his livestock. Cities of refuge were set up (Numbers 35:9-28) as sanctuary for those who inadvertently, or without premeditation, killed someone. No one could be executed on the evidence of only one witness and there were specified requirements for witnesses to a crime (Deuteronomy 19:15-21).

Jewish scholars question whether a great many of the permitted executions actually took place. Jewish nonviolence has ancient roots. Centuries before Jesus' birth a Jewish court which handed down more than one death sentence every seven years was disgraced and termed a "bloody court." Although there were seven legal means of execution, the wrongdoer was often "left to the vengeance of God."

When an execution was scheduled, the Talmud decreed that a herald precede the convicted person crying out: "X, the son of Y, is going forth to be executed because he has committed such and such an offense, and Z and W are his accusing witnesses. Whoever knows anything in defense of X, let him come and state it."

Public executions by stoning still took place occasionally in the New Testament. The possibility was at least discussed in John 8:1-12, and Stephen was stoned to death (Acts 7:58) by men whose cloaks were kept safe by Saul, later the apostle Paul. Years later, Paul himself was stoned for the crime of being a Christian, and left for dead. Fortunately, he was *not* dead, apparently not even badly injured (Acts 14:19-20).

In the earliest Old Testament books, treatment of prisoners was not a theme. Seminomadic people, like those early Israelites, usually do not take prisoners. By the sixth century before Christ, when the Psalms were beginning to be collected and recorded, there are references to the Lord delivering prisoners. For example, Psalm 146:5a and 7 tells us:

> Happy is he whose help is the God of Jacob . . . who executes justice for the oppressed; who gives food to the hungry. The Lord sets the prisoners free.

The prophets, haunted by God's demands for justice, made demands on God's people for the prisoner, along with the hungry, the oppressed, and the fatherless. Jeremiah put in some prison time himself, captive of the invading Chaldean army.

In Lamentations 3:34, 36 (NEB) we read: "To trample underfoot any prisoner in the land . . . the Lord has never approved."

The familiar Micah 6:6-8 deals unforgettably with what God actually *does* require of those who sin. (Obviously, all of us.)

> "With what shall I come before the Lord, and bow myself before God on high? Shall I come before him with burnt offerings, with calves a year old? Will the Lord be pleased with thousands of rams, with ten thousands of rivers of oil? Shall I give my first-born for my transgression, the fruit of my body for the sin of my soul?" He has showed you, O man, what is good; and what does the Lord require of you but to do justice, and to love kindness, and to walk humbly with your God?

Isaiah described the Messiah as one who would "bring out the prisoners from the dungeon, from the prison those who sit in darkness" (Isaiah 42:7). And the dramatic passage, beginning with Isaiah 61:1, the text Jesus chose for his first sermon in his hometown, Nazareth, includes:

> The Spirit of the Lord God is upon me, because the Lord has anointed me to . . . proclaim liberty to the captives, and the opening of the prison to those who are bound.

Besides proclaiming freedom to prisoners, Jesus gave his followers a very strong, specific reason to visit and minister to prisoners. "I was in prison and you came to me. . . . As you did it to one of the least of these my brethren, you did it to me" (Matthew 25:36b, 40b).

Throughout his teachings, Jesus dealt continually with the question of wrongdoing, and with reaching out to the wrongdoer to reestablish him/her in the community. When his disciples were asked why Jesus ate with "tax collectors and sinners," Jesus himself replied: "Those who are well have no need of a physician, but those who are sick. Go and learn what this means, 'I desire mercy, and not sacrifice.' For I came not to call the righteous, but sinners" (Matthew 9:12-13, with Jesus quoting from Hosea 6:6).

There was also his quotation from Psalm 118 about rehabilitation: "The very stone which the builders rejected has become the head of the corner; this was the Lord's doing, and it is marvelous in our eyes" (Mark 12:10-11).

Two important passages show Jesus dealing with people known to have committed sinful and illegal acts. The first passage is from Luke 23:39-43.

> One of the criminals who were hanged railed at him, saying, "Are you not the Christ? Save yourself and us!" But the other rebuked him, saying, "Do you not fear God, since you are under the same sentence of condemnation? And we indeed justly; for we are receiving the due reward of our deeds; but this man has done nothing wrong." And he said, "Jesus, remember me when you come into your kingdom." And he said to him, "Truly, I say to you, today you will be with me in Paradise."

The other passage is from John 8:3-11.

> And placing her in the midst, they said to him, "Teacher, this woman has been caught in the act of adultery. Now in the law Moses commanded us to stone such. What do you say about her?" This they said to test him, that they might have some charge to bring against him. Jesus bent down and wrote with his finger on the ground. And as they continued to ask him, he stood up and said to them, "Let him who is without sin among you be the first to throw a stone at her." And once more he bent down and wrote with his finger on the ground. But when they heard it, they went away, one by one, beginning with the eldest, and Jesus was left alone with the woman standing before him. Jesus looked up and said to her, "Woman, where are they? Has no one condemned you?" She said, "No one, Lord." And Jesus said, "Neither do I condemn you; go, and do not sin again."

How do these commands of Jesus affect us today? Aren't modern crime and prisons pretty messy places to get involved? The entire scene is frustrating, intensely political, confusing, and frequently brutal. Criminals turn into victims, occasionally victims into criminals.

It would be hard enough to keep a pure heart in a lethal environment like that. We certainly couldn't keep our hands clean.

Kenneth L. Carder reminds us that Christians have *been* involved, for a long time now:

> The early church counted in its membership a large number of prisoners, ex-prisoners, and other outcasts. Jesus was himself a prisoner who received the death penalty. The dominant symbol of the church is another culture's electric chair, the cross. Many of the church's sacred writings came out of prison cells.
>
> Down through the ages this "Body of Christ" has been in the forefront of prison reform. . . . The modern penitentiary is partly the creation of the church . . . seen as an alternative to maiming and physical torture. It was to be a place where offenders would be sent to meditate on their sins and come out as whole, forgiven people. But that which was created to transform criminals soon became a monster in need of change.*

Paul, who spent a lot of time in prison and claimed to find it a good place to witness to his faith, understandably empathized

*Kenneth L. Carder, "The Church and the Prisoner" *Cities* (Knoxville, Tenn., July 1981).

with prisoners and all wrongdoers who yearned for a new life. Writing to the Romans (3:10), he quoted from Psalm 14, "None is righteous, no not one."

In his letter to the Galatians (6:1) he gave specific advice on working with someone who has done wrong:

> Brethren, if a man is overtaken in any trespass, you who are spiritual should restore him in a spirit of gentleness. Look to yourself, lest you two be tempted.

In a letter to the Hebrews, the writer drew on the common heritage of the Jews, describing Jesus as their high priest, appointed by God, and sharing with them the human condition: "He can deal gently with the ignorant and wayward, since he himself is beset with weakness" (5:2).

The letter admonishes the Hebrew church to "Remember those who are in prison, as though in prison with them" (13:3a).

As we work all day at Project Return with people who have been convicted of felonies, our strongest reaction is how much alike we are. Not that most of us could possibly commit a murder, a rape, an armed robbery. (I am having trouble bringing myself to kill some mice who have moved into my kitchen!)

Nor did most of us grow up as shortchanged on loving care as did the majority of those who have been convicted of crimes. The earliest lesson many of our people learned was: If I want to survive, I have to take care of myself *any way I can.*

Nevertheless, we laugh and cry at the same things, learn to share and support each other, and develop a real sense of community—a faith community in which the gospel is mostly preached in sign language.

"Riding the Bible out of prison" is such a standard con game that prisoners of integrity are easily turned off by too rapid, too glib statements about religion. They've seen too many jailhouse conversions which last only through the parole hearing and the checkout door of the prison. While they may respect genuine faith, they learn it best in a laboratory, not in lectures.

Thomas O. Murton, who went in as superintendent to clean up the notorious Tucker Prison Farm in Arkansas, has made some observations about religion in prison which should make other Christians cringe. For example: "It is more than just coincidence that the first building destroyed at Attica (as it has been in other prison riots) was the chapel. For the prisoners, the church has become a symbol of hypocrisy."

Being safely irrelevant was not limited to the state-subsidized religion within the prison either, Murton pointed out. He told about one pastor who "became furious when I asked for literacy materials in lieu of a portion of the 300 Bibles he wanted to send to Tucker."

It had not mattered to the pastor that 40 percent of the inmates were illiterate and at least four did not know their ABCs. "The main thing was to have a Bible in each cell, whether it could be read or not."

This gives a tough challenge to those of us whose job seems to be to demonstrate our faith to people leaving prison. Looking in the mirror each morning as we dress, we are acutely aware that *all* have sinned, and none of us will make it through the day without God's help.

Constantly needing and receiving grace, we can sometimes manage to share it.

◊ TEN ◊

Prison chaplains—between God and Caesar

Harmon Wray had an appointment one day at Brushy Mountain State Prison with a brand-new chaplain.

Harmon was on time. The chaplain wasn't.

Harmon waited half an hour before he asked a guard, "What happened to the new chaplain?"

"He'll be back pretty soon," the guard said politely. "Since it's his first day, he's out doing his practice on the pistol range."

Some prison chaplains would never be found on a pistol range, no matter who suggested it. Some prison administrators would never dream of having a chaplain working on marksmanship as part of his job description. But such possibilities do exist, as long as prison chaplains are hired and paid by state and federal prison system. Some of us think they should be working for religious denominations instead.

The Internal Revenue Service has ruled that: "Services performed by an employee of a state as a chaplain in a state prison are performed by a civil servant of the state and not as a minister in the exercise of the ministry" (Publication 535, Internal Revenue Service: Self-Employment Tax).

Most prison chaplains *do* consider themselves ministers in

the exercise of a particularly difficult ministry. Their roles are confusing, though: working for God, paid by Caesar.

It takes an extraordinary chaplain to work effectively with prisoners whom his employer is keeping locked up. Occasionally, a chaplain manages by force of personality and personal faith to have a real impact on prisoners' lives. But it can't be done by professional techniques, and certainly not by using the power handed him by his job description.

There was one time in history when "the Word became flesh and *dwelt among us*." That's the only model that will work for chaplains or anyone working with prisoners. To the extent that we forsake authority and privilege and share the prisoners' actual lives, we can sometimes be of real help. And it can never be top-down help. The only magic is genuine friendship with other children of God whom we value, respect, and sometime need to help *us*.

When that occurs, it matters less who signs the paycheck, but it does matter.

One perceptive prisoner said, "The state hires chaplains to make everybody feel better about having us locked up. It's a lot like that prayer a chaplain is supposed to say just before they execute someone. It kind of makes it look like God buys the whole package."

John Howard Yoder has warned of the temptation of the church "to sanctify the power structures."

A Catholic chaplains' team in Rhode Island refused to conduct Easter masses for inmates in the Providence prison. "We would be used to lend legitimacy and blessings to a system warranting no legitimacy and blessing," Father Ronald Marstin explained for the team. Supported by their bishop, the chaplains were protesting a much narrowed definition of their ministry which the prison warden and corrections officials were trying to impose.

This ability of a denomination to back its chaplains against the state appears to be one of the most appealing things about a church-supported prison chaplaincy. Father Jim Hannon, in a paper for a Vanderbilt Divinity School course, questioned the assumption that it would happen often. He pointed out that mainline denominations have refused time and time again to stand behind even their parish ministers in controversial situations. Protestant chaplains are, in most cases, essentially isolated from their denominations, not even included in pension plans. And he asked: "When has the church ever been willing to take on the state in this country?"

In Virginia, chaplains *are* paid by their denominations, since the state of Virginia doesn't hire any prison chaplains. If other states declined to hire chaplains, I hope the churches would supply them.

I suggested once to deputy commissioner of correction Bob Morford that Tennessee quit hiring chaplains. "You're already having budget problems," I pointed out. "Shouldn't paying ministers be the responsibility of the churches?"

Some college professors consider Bob one of the brightest men in corrections. He has taken a personal, life-changing interest in a lot of long-term prisoners. His wife has, too. Recently released prisoners have told me about being invited to the Morfords' house for dinner. Bob likes to talk like a hardline organizational man, though, and he understands power.

"I don't *want* the churches to pay the prison chaplains," he said. "The Catholic chaplain is the only one now whom I can't control."

However, as the budget problems worsened in the wake of a federal court order, the DOC did decide to take most chaplains off the state payroll.

Now it was time for the churches to take action. They did. They put so much pressure on the commissioner of correction that he reversed his decision and kept the chaplains on his payroll.

Obviously, not the letter but the spirit is the important thing. How chaplains work, and the environment they work in, matters more than who signs their paychecks. After all, it would be possible for denominations to hire and pay chaplains and continue to sweep them and their ministries under the rug, along with the prisoners they work with.

Regardless of who handles the ministry within the prison, they and the people they work with are part of the body of Christ, with all the rest of us. We dare not say, "I have no need of you."

Since prisoners can't, at the moment, worship with us in our churches, we will need to go to theirs to be with them. And if administrators do not welcome Christians from outside the prisons to worship with their prisoner brothers and sisters, it will be necessary to work for some rule changes.

It is complicated to keep everyone safe, fed, and confined in an overcrowded prison. We must be considerate and tactful when we visit. But it is *our* prison. We are paying the astronomical cost to run it. Other children of God are locked up and on staff there. The church must be present also.

Practically all these prisoners will be released sooner or later, back to the "free world." We need to have a hand outstretched to welcome them home. Of course, they will need help in finding a job, a place to live, and all the rest. Who doesn't when returning from a strange country? But, mainly, they will need to be welcomed, loved, and held to account as fellow human beings—valuable and contributing people.

However prison chaplains are selected and paid, there are two things they must have to work effectively, just as any ministers anywhere must. One is the ability to be *in* the world but not *of* it—to observe the system and criticize it when necessary. The other is the ability to assure confidentiality.

"Okay, so I goofed," Joe, a twenty-year-old prisoner, told me. He had urgently requested that I come out to the prison to see him.

"I'm afraid someone's going to get hurt, though, and I need you to talk to the associate warden. He needs to move some people so they'll be safe."

Joe and several other prisoners had been gambling with free

world money. (Possession of free world money is strongly against rules. So is gambling.) Now several prisoners owed gambling debts which were likely to get them beaten up, or even fatally stabbed.

"You can't believe what some of the guys in here will do to people," Joe went on. Violence still made him sick, and he'd seen some. He needed to talk and, for a long time, I simply listened to him.

Then Joe gave me careful instructions about what to tell the assistant warden. "And forget it was me that told you," he added. "I don't need a write-up."

The assistant warden was concerned, as Joe had known he would be. He took quick, appropriate action.

Joe phoned me at the office. "Everything's cool, okay," he reported. "I don't know who might be dead if it weren't for you."

I don't want to be seen as *that* necessary. Next time someone's in jeopardy, I might be out of town.

"Couldn't one of the chaplains have handled it?" I suggested.

Joe snorted. "Maybe. Maybe not. All I know is, when I meet that parole board, I don't want to hear about this from my records."

I don't think he would have. But this prisoner's perception is a problem that prison chaplains face in doing their jobs. Prison administrators have sometimes invaded chaplains' offices and taken records for what the chaplains considered improper use. As a result, chaplains in some prisons keep few written records on prisoners. Many chaplains are also careful not to promise confidentiality since job pressures can make such a promise impossible to keep.

I've heard prison chaplains point out, though, that prisoners who don't trust state-paid chaplains would probably also distrust church-paid chaplains. It would amaze any member of the New Testament church to know that prisoners today consider the church "establishment." Few prisoners have any reason to trust the establishment.

Chaplains are considered part of the "treatment team" which makes important decisions about each prisoner. How shall a new prisoner be classified? Will he serve his time in a minimum-security work release center? Or will he be judged to need the grim restrictions of maximum security with the most dangerous prisoners in the system? Or will the most helpful approach be something in between?

What will happen when he's considered for parole? A good letter from a chaplain, or even his personal appearance at a parole hearing, can make a huge difference in a prisoner's future. That causes a lot of jailhouse conversions.

Actually, religion as a con game is apt to work much better with volunteers who occasionally come to the prison than with experienced chaplains. Chaplains are not often conned. A lot of them are continually skeptical of the people with whom they work.

A church-and-corrections committee had put together a plan, originally suggested by a chaplain, where prisoners leaving prison could request that a church sponsor them. People in the sponsoring church would visit the prisoner, and then help with job hunting, housing, family problems, and so on, when he was released.

Members of the committee, including Harmon Wray, were meeting with the chaplains at Tennessee State Prison.

One committee member reported on the screening plan. Prisoners would apply to the chaplain's office at their prison, and the chaplains would screen the applicants and pass on the recommended ones to the committee, along with some information about them to use in placement.

"Will that work all right for you out here at the main prison?" she asked.

"It doesn't matter," one of the chaplains told her. "Here at the penitentiary the men we get are really scraped off the bottom of the barrel. We won't be referring any for this program. It wouldn't be right to ask good church people to get involved with hopeless S.O.B.s like these."

Chaplains, who almost invariably have clinical pastoral education training, usually specialize in counseling, and obviously think they can make a difference.

They are charged with the responsibility of telling prisoners about family deaths, serious illnesses, and other catastrophes, and they help communicate with prisoners' families.

They spend a big chunk of their time making arrangements for other ministers to work in the prison. It is possible that this liaison work and scheduling could be done by someone else, not necessarily a minister.

But if the present state-paid chaplains were replaced by church-paid chaplains, we'd need to be sure we still had good access to the prisons and prisoners.

The ability to criticize the system is essentially the job of a *prophet*. There seems no valid way to minister to someone if you can't critique and try to change the things that oppress that person.

The Hebrew prophets were usually *outside* the power structure but *inside* the national community. And this double-sided identity was crucial—both parts of it.

Even in the presumably free world, it can be difficult to be simultaneously prophet and pastor. As one minister asked, "If I were demonstrating at the Pentagon, who would see Ruth Amory through her heart surgery?"

A *Manual for Religious Services* published by the Tennessee Department of Correction, with help from the American Correctional Association and the California Department of Correction, gives some interesting insights on the ambiguities.

A list of "six distinct contributions the chaplain can make to the correctional program" is a surprise because it's a good list. It starts out:

> (1) He should promote the fact that each person is an individual made in God's image for a purpose and with worth.
> (2) He is to bring the message of redeeming love to a situation where there is still a great deal of cynicism, punitiveness, and despair, and so on, constructive to the end.

It almost surprises you to read in the same manual: "The chaplain will be expected to provide a written summary of religious information concerning each inmate, which will become part of his permanent file"; and, "None of the regulations of the Department of Correction should ever be in conflict with religious principles. The chaplain will obey them in the spirit of good will and cooperation."

The manual gives no instructions for chaplains facing the death penalty with an inmate. With so many states bent on legalized judicial murder, this seems a serious omission. It also underlines why it is urgent that chaplains be working for the church, not for Caesar. It is reasonable for a pastor to be with one of his people facing death. It is not reasonable for him to be there as part of the team putting the person to death.

◊ E L E V E N ◊

Hilarious giving—investing in miracles

> The point is this: he who sows sparingly will also reap sparingly, and he who sows bountifully will also reap bountifully. Each one must do as he has made up his mind, not reluctantly or under compulsion, for God loves a *hilarious* giver. And God is able to provide you with every blessing in abundance, so that you may always have enough of everything and may provide in abundance for every good work. 2 Corinthians 9:6-8.

We changed one word in the Revised Standard translation. Ted Brown, formerly at Vanderbilt Divinity School, liked the translation (reasonable from the Greek), *hilarious giver*.

We like it, too. Hilarious givers build community. Top-down givers create hostility. Some of the people we work with have had a lot of practice in feeling hostile, and we certainly don't want to trigger more hostility.

The prodigal son's father was a hilarious giver. He was not conned nor manipulated. Paying little attention to the self-serving confession his son had planned, he welcomed the boy home exuberantly and *chose* to give him gifts. Most people we welcome home from prison have needs more urgent than a fatted calf, but those of us who welcome them should remember that biblical model of hilarious giving.

Hilarious giving makes the people we are working with responsible receivers. That used to startle us, too, but we've learned to expect it.

The whole staff was shaken up the day Richard Lyons struggled up the office steps on crutches to pay back ten dollars he felt he owed us.

He had served forty years in prison for burglaries and a murder, long ago when he was wild and young. He had finally been released, largely because of serious heart disease and diabetes.

The first time he came to the office, he just wanted help finding an apartment. He was getting about three hundred dollars a month in disability and thought he could manage nicely on that. However, I discovered that his check was late that month because of a change of address. Richard's human services worker had assured him that he'd get it in a couple of days.

With his diabetes, it would have been dangerous to skip any meals and the late check worried me. "What are you doing for lunch?" I asked. "I'm sending out for sandwiches."

Over his protests, I bought his lunch. It became pretty evident that he had not had breakfast and I wasn't sure he'd eaten much the day before.

Another staff member drove Richard to the public housing office, trying to expedite getting him into a high-rise apartment for the elderly and handicapped. Then they stopped by the food bank to pick up an emergency food box. I also gave Richard ten dollars and asked him to phone me so I could be sure his check got there on time.

He didn't phone, and the housing people couldn't locate him when a vacant apartment turned up. We drove by his house but he didn't seem to be there. The city hospitals and the jail hadn't heard from him, nor had his parole officer.

"Maybe he just found an apartment and moved," someone suggested, and we hoped that was the story. He should have gotten his parole officer's permission before moving, though. We were bothered, and a little irritated, but there didn't seem to be anything else we could do right then.

More than two months later, Richard struggled into the office on crutches.

Mamie rushed to help him into a chair. "What happened to you?"

"Broke my hip. I was out in the country so they put me in a hospital out there."

"When did you get out of the hospital?"

"Oh, couple of hours ago. I just rode the suburban bus in. Owe you all ten dollars and wanted to pay it. The hospital social worker got my check sent out there, so I have the money."

By now, everyone was in the front office, clustered around him.

"Where does that suburban bus stop?" Bob asked quietly.

"Not far. Five or six blocks from here. You can't believe how slow I was walking that little old distance."

I *could* believe it. "Whatever it takes, get him a comfortable bed," I instructed a couple of staff members. "Try the housing office. See if anyone will take him in. If necessary, get a church to pay for a hotel room."

"If nothing else works, we'll pass the hat in here and skip lunch for the week," Bob agreed grimly.

But another long termer, Gene Barber, who had served most of the forty years with Richard, heard of his plight. He wasn't much younger, but a lot healthier, and we'd gotten him a job as a church custodian.

"I have an apartment," he said, coming by our office after work, "and there will always be a place for Richard wherever I am."

We gave them a ride home and put some extra groceries in their refrigerator. Like any other people who have faced hazards together for a long time, long-term prisoners can form very good friendships.

This is something parole people need to keep in mind when

they make rules against "associating with other ex-convicts." You don't, of course, want several people leaving prison to take an apartment together as a headquarters for armed robberies or drug pushing. That happens occasionally and needs to be firmly handled. But far more often, prison friendships, especially friendships of men who have served many years together, are the kind of good friendships all of us find life giving. Lonely men leaving prison need them as desperately as oxygen.

We practically never loan money. The chances are too good that the person will find it humanly impossible to repay on schedule. We don't like setting up failures, and allowing people to feel irresponsible. Nor do we want to lose a friend because he owes us, and doesn't have, five dollars.

If someone insists on planning to repay the money we've found (for busfare to work until payday, an urgent prescription, or required safety-toed boots), I suggest handling it differently:

"We don't make loans. As soon as you get ahead a little, we'd be glad to receive a contribution. In fact, if you get rich, we'd love lots of contributions."

We gave Harold twenty dollars for boots for his new construction job. Bob had made arrangements with the store to sell the boots for a fraction of their usual price.

Exactly two weeks later, Harold brought us fifty dollars. "This is to help someone else start a new job."

I protested. He'd just gotten his first paycheck.

He laughed and showed me his paycheck stub for the two-week period. He had averaged eighty hours a week and made a great deal more money than I do. We gratefully accepted his contribution.

Few of our people ever prosper as quickly as Harold, but a surprising number of them drop by the office with gifts to help someone else. It may be part of their income tax refund, the coins they've saved in their penny jar, or the money saved by skipping a couple of beers. Some money is a lot more valuable than other money. The most valuable money we see are those hard-earned contributions which say thank-you by helping someone else.

When people (usually just out of prison) *need* money, that same responsible attitude often shows up. We know the people we are working with, and use carefully the money entrusted to us, but we avoid checking out every word they say. People are more likely to be worthy of trust when they feel trusted.

I know one agency that sends people home for a year's rent receipts before issuing a ten- or twenty-dollar food order. That costs $1.40 in bus fare plus hours of time *if* they have—and can find—rent receipts. It's easy for a social agency to get tied up in knots like that, but it's not cost-effective.

And being checked up on is a challenge to ingenuity. "I can't believe a word those people tell me" is the accurate complaint of a staff member in an agency that operate through distrust.

It works better to plan with each person how they and we together can manage to keep them alive until they have a payday or two. Did they manage to save any money while they were in prison? Amazing if they did. Top prison pay is $55 a month in Tennessee (to cover clothes and toilet articles, plus radio, books, birthday gifts for the kids, cigarettes, whatever it took to make life behind walls somewhat bearable). For the majority of prisoners, no job was available, and if there was no job, there was no pay.

Have they applied for emergency food stamps until their paydays start? What about housing, transportation to work, and clothes? Does this job require anything special: a cosmetology license renewed, uniforms, tools, or safety equipment? How, working together, can we get these essentials?

Project Return is visibly not very rich. Embarrassing (but accurate) rumors drift around the prisons that the staff is occasionally paid late. This probably has something to do with the extreme thrift of most of the people we work with. We constantly learn money-saving tricks from some of them which we can pass on to others.

Sometimes I think they're underestimating their minimum needs. It's expensive and complicated to face a crisis without even the price of a phone call.

"Look," I sometimes tell them. "Here's five dollars from petty cash to stick in the back of your billfold in case you have an emergency. You can return it after you get paid."

Sometimes they take it, but "I don't need that" is the frequent response. "Look," one of them told me, emptying a coin purse on my desk."I still have nearly two dollars and all these pennies—and Friday I get my food stamps."

I don't suppose this same dynamic would work for an agency with a million-dollar endowment and mahogany furniture, but I do believe it would work better than the grudging style sometimes used when giving help. A good staff should be able to judge the appropriateness of requests for up to twenty dollars without elaborate checking. If you know what you're doing, it is usually fairly easy to tell whether or not someone is telling you the truth. You know whether the names are right, the places are right, the story jibes with the surrounding stories that are so familiar. Hours of phone calls use a lot of valuable time and do very little for a staff's batting average. If the staff is good, the money is mostly well spent. If it's not, elaborate checking won't help much.

You don't give cash to someone who will probably spend it for liquor instead of lunch; you might take him out for a sociable hamburger instead.

If you're recommending someone for a job or entrance into an expensive training program, of course you check references. It's best done with the person present. If all the references are terrible (fortunately, unusual), you have one kind of problem that you need to attack together. If most are good but one strategic one is bad, both of you need to understand why and plan together how to handle it.

Before you can *give* money responsibly, it's necessary to *get* money responsibly. Perhaps the majority of nonprofit groups in the United States which work with prisoners began during the lifetime of the Law Enforcement Assistance Act agency. Others have been spawned by federal programs like CETA, or the social justice budgets of religious denominations. There was a lot of speculation in print that job programs for people leaving prison died with LEAA but the smaller, quieter, and more effective church-related programs mostly continue business as usual.

People often choose to work in corrections precisely because they are interested in helping people. Many of them are very effective. Wardens, parole officers, guards, and the parole board have clearly defined jobs which everyone understands. Part of their job description is to protect the public by keeping a prisoner securely locked up. Another part is to help the prisoner get his life into shape so things will be better when he is released.

Considering that the goals are somewhat contradictory, it's impressive how well many people in the area do their jobs. But people like chaplains and volunteer coordinators are supposed to be working with and for the prisoners and their families. That's hard to manage when you're hired and paid by the Department of Correction. Prisoners respect a warden who is both tough and concerned, but they are confused by the prison system's official do-gooders.

Ken Walker called long distance. He had not reported to his parole officer for several months and had been out of state without permission. It began when his father fell critically ill and he couldn't reach his parole officer by phone before catching the first bus to Mississippi.

Then a part-time job turned up, near enough to his parents' home. Ken took it so he could help nurse his recovering father. By now, he was already in serious parole violation and afraid to phone his parole officer. It took several months for Ken to get up the nerve even to phone me.

We had worked with Ken a long time and had a generally good opinion of him. Knowing that his specific parole officer was fair and understanding, I suggested that Ken phone him directly.

Ken was afraid to. His father was better and he was willing to come back to Tennessee and return to his old job, if his employer would have him back. He was frightened, though, about being sent back to prison.

I agreed to make some phone calls. Ken had been an excellent employee and his boss was pleased that he could come back to work. That helped a lot.

With Ken's job secure and his otherwise good record, his parole officer was willing to give him another chance. Ken did have to pay up the monthly ten-dollar compensation fund payments he had skipped while he was out of state.

Situations like this come up fairly often when you're working in the prison area. It's easy to see why the prisoner finds it easier to trust you when you aren't on a government payroll.

There are big advantages to local funding. The money goes further. While you certainly need good accounting and auditing procedures any time you are handling public funds, they cost much less if you aren't under government guidelines. Twenty percent or more of a federal grant is often used in accounting for how it's spent.

Small agencies with little time for bookkeeping find themselves bogged down with myriad forms and regulations, mostly really intended for much larger, richer organizations. Internal Revenue is usually the greatest obstacle. A new agency will need to laboriously establish its nonprofit status with the IRS so gifts to the agency are tax deductible. Then there will be payroll tax to deposit, 990 tax forms to fill out annually, quarterly reports, and a lot of correspondence spewed out of IRS computers to deal with.

If the federal government is really interested in encouraging volunteers and nonprofit agencies, they might start with the IRS. Friendly, well-trained nonprofit specialists could steer a new agency through the first steps and conceivably even offer help on occasional financial problems not directly related to submitting payments which IRS insists are overdue.

That would be concrete evidence that the federal government is sincere in encouraging private charity, and a good opening gambit for improving the IRS image in the land. It would also amaze agency bookkeepers.

Local money comes with a vital fringe benefit—local interest. Besides sending us checks to keep the office running, people in Nashville call us about jobs and drop by with cookies to serve with our ever-perking coffee.

People remember us in their prayers, give us their bunk beds when the kids outgrow them, and invite us to speak to their church and civic groups.

"Invest in a miracle" we urge and, as the Scriptures say, where they invest their treasure, their hearts are also. We couldn't begin to do our jobs without all their support.

◇ T W E L V E ◇

Jobs for *all* our futures

Everyone in the personnel department of a Nashville iron-works, as well as Project Return's staff, has gotten a lift from J. D. Greene, whom the governor released on clemency a year ago.

Too often the breaks in court and prison go only to the middle-class defendant or prisoner, the one who's had special privileges all his life. In our experience, these are rarely the ones who make the best use of a break.

J. D. almost didn't get out. The parole board had recommended clemency, but his papers lay unsigned in the governor's office for ten whole months. When someone at Project Return called to ask about them, an aide to the governor sounded hesitant.

"The governor really hasn't decided," she said slowly. "We hate to turn him down, but there's so little reason to think he'll do well—no job experience, almost no education, no family."

"We might be able to fill in a little for the family," our staff member said, "and we *can* help him get a job."

I don't know how much that low-key promise affected the decision, but soon after that J. D. was released.

He'd been locked up since his teens and the governor's office wasn't exaggerating his complete lack of job experience. He was bright and attractive, though, and tall with dark brown skin and good features. He seemed like a guy you would naturally trust.

I stopped to wish him well as Bob was sending him out to an ironworks for an interview.

"Look, J. D.," I told him. "You need a good reference more than anything, even money in the bank. I want you to land that job and be the best employee these people have ever had. If you can manage that, we can help you figure out how to get a lot of the other things you want."

I've probably said similar things to a lot of job hunters, but none ever took me more literally than J. D. He got the job, and in a couple of weeks, we had a phone call from the personnel manager. "J. D.'s the best new employee we've had for years," she said. "Got any more like him?"

"Well, *almost* as good," Bob Hill said judiciously, picking out a job seeker to send her.

Within the next year, we placed twenty people at that ironworks, thanks to J. D.

Sometimes he stops by to thank us and we point out, accurately, that it is *we* who need to be doing the thanking. We and the other employees for whose jobs he's responsible.

He shakes his head at that. "No one ever even thought I could do well before," he invariably tells us.

"How's life going *off* the job, J. D.?" I asked one day. I knew Bob had helped him find an apartment.

His smile broadened. "I have a job I like and the boss says I'm good. I have a nice place to live. I have friends, and you people are always glad to see me. If there's anything I want real bad, I can save up the money and get it. Nobody ever told me life could be this nice."

We love seeing his joy, but one thought bothers us. His thrills are things most of us have always considered givens.

It's more exciting to be an armed robber than a dishwasher. When a young person comes out of prison, anxious to finally build a good future, it is chilling to be hastily processed into a dead-end job. He's told, sometimes in so many words: "Okay, this is *your* job. You should be all set. Go be a good citizen!"

An endless future of dull, menial work, with few attainable dreams for the future isn't very attractive. This is especially true if your friends think more of armed robbers than they do of people like dishwashers.

I am officially "very stable" and I've had breaks in the past which should make me good at handling life. I am aware, though, that I couldn't handle being released from prison in a strange city, with almost no money, no friends or family, and no one to laugh with me if I get a job or cry with me if someone slams the door again. Having some bureaucrat hastily slip me into a dull, menial job slot would help very little.

How about you? Try to imagine yourself twenty-one again. You've been in prison three years and your hometown really doesn't want you back. You wish they did, but you're really not surprised. They didn't want you when you were a kid, either. You're being paroled to Nashville with thirty dollars, a new pair of jeans, a sweatshirt, *and* a prison record.

You had to line up a job and a place to stay before they'd approve your parole plan. You're a little uneasy about them, but hoping they work out. They don't.

It's been a long time since you had any family. You pretty much raised yourself on the street. In Nashville, you don't know one person who's not locked up. For a minute, you kind of wish you were still locked up with them.

The rain is cold and, shivering, you realize you don't own a jacket. That one with TSP (Tennessee State Prison) on the back you never intended to wear again so you left it.

You never had much of a job *before* you were locked up. You stacked lumber a few days, and washed dishes in a fast-food place.

You see a restaurant up the street. Maybe *they* need a dishwasher. You're cold, hungry, and scared, so you decide to have supper first—a good supper, although the thirty dollars is disappearing so fast it scares you.

After you eat, you talk to the manager. You tell him the truth. You don't lie. You don't want to *ever* lie again. He listens just a minute, then points to the door. "Do you know how many people have asked me for jobs today who *haven't* gotten themselves in prison? GET OUT OF HERE!"

You make yourself try two more places. One manager is nice and even gives you a cup of coffee, but he doesn't expect to have any openings. The other has "problems enough without an ex-con ripping off the place."

You manage to find Job Service but there must be 150 people waiting. You get the feeling every one of them can tell you just got out of prison. One man confides in you that he's applied at Job Service every day for two months. A secretary mentions some place called Project Return.

It's raining harder when you go out and you're cold. This Project Return is in a church and it would *not* be a good day for someone to ask, "Brother, are you saved?"

What things would you need about now? What *would* it be a good day for?

James Q. Wilson in *Thinking About Crime* pointed out that a variety of job programs for former prisoners did very little to reduce crime, even though they often included counseling, job preparation, and sometimes a paycheck while learning.

He found work release programs no more useful in reducing crime.

Wilson, a Harvard professor of government, is sometimes termed *hard on crime*. Since I run a program which views people who have been convicted of crimes as valuable human beings with futures, I am sometimes termed *soft on crime*.

One thing we don't disagree on at all are most government-funded job programs, and work release.

There are two basic problems: (1) what the job programs are trying to do, and (2) how well they do it.

One general type of program is somewhat like Job Service. The emphasis is on the job and finding someone to fill it. Outside of going over a brief summary of the applicant's training and experience, there's not much attempt to get involved with the person. This kind of program rarely includes any follow-up or troubleshooting after placement.

For someone just out of prison, personal problems can be overwhelming: chaotic housing (or none at all), painful loneliness, lack of long-range planning, overuse of alcohol and other drugs, and lack of constructive, important friendships. The chance is slim of being able to make it on a new job while trying to cope, singlehandedly, with all the other problems.

Then there's the nitty-gritty. How do you get to work until your first payday? How do you obtain the required uniform or safety equipment the boss mentions so casually?

The second kind of program, job preparation and training, is more likely to deal with the personal problems. CETA ran a lot of programs like this. So did the Manpower Demonstration Research Corporation.

The big drawback seems to be that few participants in these programs ever wind up in a plain everyday job with a plain everyday paycheck.

The people we work with who have been through these programs have usually learned to put together a résumé, somewhat misspelled. Their expectations have increased considerably, usually more than their skills.

The programs which seemed most disastrous to me were those described by Wilson where: "all the participants in a given work setting were people with problems; thus the difficulties experienced by people with chronic employment problems when they find themselves competing with persons who are successful job-seekers and job-holders were minimized."

When you put "chronic employment problems" together and give them a fairly sophisticated task to do, the results are rarely impressive. Frequently, they are terrible.

That's hardly surprising. These programs have supervisors who do have job skills, but rarely the unusual abilities required to meld their inexperienced workers into an effective team. Besides, all too frequently there just isn't much work done.

Some new job programs have a built-in job placement requirement for the contractor. The contractor does not get full pay for training any applicant until that applicant is placed in a job and holds it for thirty days.

That should help, and it might help still more to have additional incentives for applicant, contractor, and employer if the applicant stays on the job six months and is then retained as a permanent employee.

Besides problems with program design, a second basic problem is that a lot of programs are just not very well done. Though the forest may look good, the individual trees are rarely handled with skill and care. It takes continual hard work to know the employers and job market in an area, and also be deeply involved with applicants and know their strengths, weaknesses, and hopes. Too often, nobody works that hard.

We've had particularly good experience with the tax credits given employers for hiring former prisoners and other hard-to-place applicants. They involve placement in real jobs, in normal work situations, with enough subsidy for the employer at first to cover a little additional training and supervision. A promising employee is apt to have a permanent job at the end of that three-year period during which he's been a tax bargain.

An unpromising employee will be unemployed again long before the three years is up. This is true of all government job programs. An occasional person, with or without a prison record, may have physical and mental handicaps so severe that only in a sheltered workshop, closely supervised and subsidized, will he ever be able to work successfully. These valuable workshops for the handicapped, however, are not the job programs we are discussing.

Only a minority of former prisoners have serious permanent job handicaps. The majority of people leaving prison make good employees if they are skillfully placed and trained, and if someone deals effectively with any problems that come up.

If the job applicant has been locked up since his teens, and has had little experience or education, the first job will usually be routine, dull, and not too well paid. The employee has the right to understand this and certainly to understand that this job is a necessary temporary step toward his/her future goals.

"What you want from this job," we sometimes explain, "is money to eat on for six months, plus a really good reference. You want that employer to be standing there, with big tears in his eyes, when you leave for a better job."

Just getting to work regularly and on time, and doing a dull job creditably, rates compliments and support. A prisoner has been herded around, whenever and wherever someone else decides, usually with no chance to take responsibility for his own life.

If problems do come up on a new job, our employers often call Project Return's job developers and let them try to work things out. By then, they've probably also gotten an appeal for help from the employee.

Our job developers are creative about getting free world jobs on the basis of prison experience.

Gerald, coming out after a long sentence beginning as a teenager, asked if we could find him a job somewhere cleaning up.

"No free world job experience," he explained briefly.

"You haven't been in the free world since you were old enough to work. What did you do inside?" Robert Arnold asked, leaning back in his chair to make it clear he had plenty of time to listen.

In his twenty years in prison, Gerald had done a lot of things. What he'd done most, and liked best, was cooking. He'd liked the challenges of trying to make something really good out of prison fare, and as a reward he'd done real gourmet cooking for a time, working in the governor's mansion.

With a little salesmanship, Robert soon got Gerald a trial assignment as a cook for a motel chain. Four months later, he was head cook, helping to interview applicants we sent over.

Job developers have to know the people they are working with really well and be able to spot handicaps as well as abilities. Specific criminal convictions naturally can be handicaps. Any drug conviction makes it impossible to get a job anywhere in the health field. Any sex offense removes the possibility of working with young people, and most convictions for sex offenses also make housing difficult. Most halfway houses have recently become coeducational, in the wake of the woman's liberation movement, and no longer will take anyone who has had a sex-related crime. This makes it tough to find a place for the man leaving prison who has changed his life completely since that youthful disaster twelve years earlier.

A conviction for embezzling means, as common sense would suggest, that no one wants you to handle money anymore. People who *could* embezzle were usually in jobs which required accounting or banking skills, and they've made it necessary to change fields entirely.

No one with a prison record should want to work somewhere like a bank and they probably wouldn't be hired there. Our concern is not that temptation will cause our people to get into trouble, but that routine discrepancies will look very different if someone is on hand who has served prison time.

Experienced employers have learned to expect an increase in employee theft if other employees know a former prisoner has been hired. People feel safe in ripping the business off, assuming the ex-convict will automatically be blamed. For that reason, as well as protecting the former prisoner's privacy, the employer usually doesn't allow the prison record to be discussed.

Our reputation for effective job placement occasionally causes problems. An attractive black teenager came to the office one day, seeking a job. Not much over five feet, he looked nearer fifteen than the nineteen he claimed, but he was bright, ambitious, and energetic. He had *almost* everything we need in a job applicant—everything but a criminal conviction.

"Someone will really like hiring you," I explained gently, "but we're not the right place to help you. You need to go to Job

Service. We only work with people who have been in prison or are on probation."

"You mean Project Return only gets people jobs who have committed crimes?" he asked, disappointed.

I nodded.

He thought a minute. Then his face brightened. "I'll be back in half an hour," he said.

I bent the rules enough to give him a few suggestions about places to apply. There should be more help available to a promising youngster like this.

Work release is a good idea that rarely works very well. Rather than spending prison time in mind-numbing idleness, the prisoner is allowed to hold an outside job for wages. He is then charged for room and board and the victims' compensation fund. He may even have a little left to send his family, and to handle his own personal expenses.

Counselors are supposed to help find work release jobs, but the amount of help actually given depends on the counselor. There are restrictions on how freely the prisoner can go job hunting, and he runs into even more questions from employers than people do who have just been released from prison. Employers sometimes are hesitant because of previous experience with work release.

We've had work release employees at Project Return. Occasionally, they just don't show up. Eventually, late in the morning, we'll get a phone call.

"I've been in a long line for the phone for hours. They won't let us out today. There was an escape last night." (Or maybe it was a fight, or perhaps his counselor wants to see him.)

Sometimes work release prisoners are allowed to drive cars, although it's almost impossible for them to afford. Sometimes they can get to work on city buses. But because of the isolated spots where prisons are built, many have to rely on transportation supplied by the work release center for a fee. Tennessee prisoners call these "chain cars."

Sometimes the chain cars get prisoners to work late. Sometimes they get them back to the work release center after check-in time—which means a disciplinary write-up.

For certain kinds of rough labor, some employers like work release. Except for the rare days when they can't come at all, a truckload of "hands" are delivered to do the dirty work: loading lumber in a lumberyard, doing first aid on asphalt roads, picking farm crops, and so on. There's no problem with individuals being late or absent, and it's hard for them to quit work.

An occasional prisoner starts a job on work release which continues to work out for him/her after release from prison. This is rare; work release jobs and free world jobs usually just aren't the same.

Federal prisoners usually spend their last ninety days in a halfway house in the area where they are going to live, on work release. This sometimes works out better. The work release idea has a lot of merit; it's worth being handled better than most prison systems are handling it.

The most valuable training prisoners get inside most prisons is helping run the prison.

"A lot of free world people in prison administration couldn't handle their jobs without the help of their convict clerk," one very bright prisoner, serving over three hundred years, told me once. "He's been there much longer and knows the system much better. That can give the clerk a lot of power."

A tight personnel budget can also mean that prisoners do jobs they would never have the chance to do outside. The prison prefers to use a plumber, teacher, nurse, or sign painter already trained and experienced outside. If no one with the right experience is serving time, though, it's necessary to train someone.

Little thought is given inside prison to free world uses of job skills required. I've known really skillful physician's assistants who would have qualified for excellent jobs after release, except that their convictions for rape and armed robbery meant they couldn't be licensed.

People who learn inside to be electricians, crane operators, or drug counselors can get jobs outside doing those things. One of our best job developers had worked his way up to chief inmate counselor while he was serving a long prison sentence.

The value of vocational training inside prisons depends on who is teaching it and the equipment available. Occasionally, it's excellent. Often it involves learning outdated jobs on outdated equipment. A program that should be useful, like keypunch, is frequently not quite good enough. Prison-trained keypunch operators test about ten strokes too slow to be hired. It would be easy to arrange things so they took the course a little longer, or a little nearer the time of their release.

There is a trend, opposed for years by labor unions which understandably worry about competition from cheap prison labor, toward genuine industry in prisons. Prisoners would do the work, be paid for it, and learn actual skills in the process.

The Scandinavian countries pioneered the idea and their prisons run commercial operations. Work for their prisoners is genuine, paid, and mandatory. It probably should be said that Scandinavian prisons have other constructive features: furloughs home for most prisoners, a much friendlier style between guards and prisoners, required savings accounts so the prisoner will leave prison with a nest egg, and excellent education and vocational training. Unfortunately, their recidivism rate doesn't seem significantly lower than ours.

The Soviet Union appears to make a profit off prison industry. Texas manages to pay a large share of the costs of its prison system by profits from prison industry. The prisoners themselves are generally not paid in Texas. There is evidence that a prison system that pays off raises the odds on people being sent to prison. This is something to think about as we set up prison industrial programs. They are a good idea with possible built-in hazards and we need to monitor them closely.

Harmon Wray suggested some of the hazards in this historical scenario:

> After the Civil War, the white power structure needed to do two things in the Confederate states: (1) reestablish white dominance over recently freed slaves so as to control the black population, and (2) develop a large pool of cheap labor to attract Northern capital and to man the factories of the Industrial Revolution in the so-called "New South."
>
> Immediately after the Civil War ended, the percentage of blacks in Tennessee State Prison rose dramatically from 33% in 1865, to 58% in 1867, then to 64% in 1869. In 1866, the practice of convict-leasing began in Tennessee, whereby the state rented out its prisoners to work for private industries at a low rate, especially in coal mining, farming, and railroads. About this same time, vaguely-worded laws were passed against "vagrancy," "loitering," and "public drunkenness." These made it easier to lock up more and more poor folks—most conveniently black—to work the mills of private industry.
>
> In 1896, convict-leasing was abolished by the legislature because of pressure from labor unions. In 1897, Brushy Mountain State Prison opened near the site where convict-leased mining operations had been going on for thirty years. And the prisoners were still mining coal, only now for the state in state-owned mines.*

There is no reason why prison industry has to create slave labor. It has the potential of teaching prisoners jobs that they can do proudly and profitably. A well-run industry should make profits and pay prisoners. They could pay for their own room and board, toiletries and clothes. They could help support their families and make at least token payments toward restitution for their victims. And we might adopt the Danish system of mandatory savings, a nest egg for their return to the community.

Nobody chooses crime for a job as they choose being a doctor, a truck driver, or a ballet dancer. Just needing money badly rarely causes crime in a direct sense, although it *can* cause desperation, and desperation can cause crime.

But having a job you can do proudly, and your friends will respect, is a vital part of putting together a good life. Good job placement can help keep people from resorting to crime again.

---

*From a lecture at Vanderbilt Divinity School. Information mostly taken from Randall G. Shelden, "From Slave to Caste Society," *Tennessee Historical Quarterly* (Winter, 1979), pp. 462-478.

◊ THIRTEEN ◊

Lord, make us an instrument of thy peace

—for the next 20 minutes, anyway

Regardless of what our constantly ringing phones interrupt, staff members' voices are warm as they answer them. Have you ever found yourself on the street with thirty dollars, a suit of clothes, and a prison record? The people we work with have and, when they call Project Return, they are often grabbing for a lifeline.

This July afternoon, though, my concern was focused on our staff. We needed a retreat, a vacation, a miracle, *something*. We'd been working too much overtime. We'd dealt with too much daily desperation.

And this last phone call was from the warden. Thomas Cantrell, who had served 39 years in prison, had terminal lung cancer.

"The parole board would like to give him a chance to live free for the couple of months he's got left," the warden explained. "He has no family left, though, except one elderly aunt in a nursing home in California. He'd need money to live on, someone to take care of him. We wondered if Project Return—"

We talked it over in staff meeting. We work as a team; decisions are made together. This one didn't take long.

I reviewed the details. In a month or two, Thomas would begin drawing disability. Otherwise, everything would be up to us: finding an apartment, scrounging for furniture, arranging medical and nursing care, and money to live on until the disability started. He'd need help with grocery shopping, laundry, cleaning, and transportation. And, most vital, he'd have to have friends, a community. Except for the faraway aunt, his family was dead, his friends all in prison.

"Don't forget," I added conscientiously, "we'll have fifty other people this month, about twenty jobs to get in this tight job market, and emergencies with the prison families."

"But if we *don't* do it, he'll die in prison," a couple of people chorused. Everyone nodded agreement.

So *whether* was no longer the question, but *how*. I assigned Karen Graham, our summer field worker from Vanderbilt Divinity School, to coordinate the project. We knew she was compassionate, responsible, and creative. We didn't know then that she also works miracles.

Finding an apartment for Thomas was the hardest thing—but Karen found one. She arranged for eight Nashville churches to contribute furniture and money for him to live on, until his disability checks started. She had a phone installed, and most important, arranged for medical care and enlisted the aid of Alive Hospice to provide a visiting nurse and a volunteer to visit Thomas regularly.

The day Thomas was released, Karen had food in his refrigerator, fresh linens on his bed, and had even arranged with a nearby drugstore to fill a prison prescription for pain pills on Saturday afternoon. With one of our board members, she went to help him through the prison checkpoint gate and to his new apartment.

The first couple of weeks were fun. Thonas had just finished radiation treatments and felt good enough to love being a free man.

"I just walked out of my apartment and kept going, any direction I wanted to walk," he reported gleefully.

Karen and her family took him along for services at Edgehill United Methodist Church, and people from Edgehill started visiting him.

For Thomas's sixty-fifth birthday, we had a party at the office, complete with a chocolate-nut cake Tara Seeley, one of our job developers, had baked. We all helped blow out the candles.

"First birthday party I ever had," Thomas said smiling. "Now as soon as I get my strength back a little, I need to go fishing. Then I'll be content."

Just then I was called to the telephone, which meant a prisoner was calling. All my other calls were being held, but we always talk to prisoners. They have a really hard time getting a telephone to use.

This was Dave Brenner, a long-termer whose name I had heard, although I had never met him. He sounded excited. "The governor's granted me clemency and I'll get out in about two weeks," he said. "I'll be needing you to help me get a job."

He hesitated a minute. "I may have to have a bypass operation first, though. They say my heart's acting up. Mainly, I just called so you'll know I'll be coming by. I've been in twenty-seven years, and ten years ago when they gave me a chance outside, I blew it. I'm going to need help. Maybe I can be some help to you all, too."

I congratulated him, and wrote his release date on the office calendar. Sometimes long-termers are very special people. Because they've been through such tough experiences, their own wrongdoing and years of punishment, they've had to look deep inside themselves. I was genuinely looking forward to meeting Dave. But heart surgery! Oh, no, not another one!

I hurried back to the birthday party. The gift Thomas had asked for, and liked most, was a soldering iron to fix his stereo. He'd built the stereo himself in prison, and it was his most prized possession—his only possession besides a few clothes.

"It was a real good day and I thank you," Thomas said as we drove him back to his apartment and fixed him a quick supper.

But that was about the last of the good days. Although he

tried to eat, and conscientiously walked around the apartment to try to keep his strength up, Thomas lost nine pounds in the next two weeks. Every bone and vein stood out. Soon he looked like the elderly father of the Thomas we had met just a month before. The doctor prescribed stronger pain pills; the Alive Hospice nurse began coming practically every day.

"Ever see a moose with a wolf after it?" Thomas asked Karen one day. "At first, a moose is too tough for a wolf to get close to, but that wolf chases the moose day and night. The moose can't eat. The moose can't sleep. By and by, the moose gives up, just stops in its tracks, and lets the wolf attack."

Then he added, very matter-of-factly, "People get like that, too."

Consciousness of approaching death seriously depressed Thomas. He was full of surprises; we discovered he'd done some preaching as a young man. He knew about Jesus and forgiveness. Nothing in his theology, though, made him think God was about to forgive two murders.

We talked about grace, but mainly we tried to make God's love show in things we did. Sometimes words aren't good enough.

Dave Brenner was released and promptly came to see us. His wife had suddenly needed emergency surgery, so he had postponed his own bypass operation. We couldn't do much for him right then except listen and be friends. We did give him one small loan which he promptly repaid.

Dave also had a birthday soon after release from prison but he was luckier than Thomas. Even with his wife in the hospital, his family got together to help him celebrate. He brought his gifts to show us, mostly fishing gear which he'd dreamed of for years.

"Hey, maybe Dave could take Thomas fishing!" I said, halfway kidding.

"Who's Thomas?" Dave demanded eagerly, wanting all the details. We told him, adding that the fishing trip was not likely to really work out.

"I know Thomas!" Dave said, excited. "We worked together

in the woodshop for years. I wondered what happened to him—you don't always hear in the joint."

He thought a minute. "We could find a nice, quiet pier and stack some pillows up for him. He could fish a little. I really do want to take him."

"Why don't you go see him then?" I suggested. "It's fun to plan a fishing trip, even if somehow it never comes off."

He visited Thomas that very day. They decided to go fishing the next morning. Hastily, I found a volunteer to go along, a strong young man who had worked in an emergency room. If Thomas needed lifting, it would be too much for Dave's heart. That fishing trip just *could* work out, I told myself happily at bedtime.

But during the night Karen was awakened by a phone call. A teenage burglar had broken into Thomas's apartment and stolen his stereo and some things from the kitchen, taunting Thomas about his helplessness.

Karen and her husband, Bill, hurried over. Thomas was not at all well. The loss of that prized stereo, plus the frustration of being a helpless victim, had been too much.

They called the police and got the apartment back in order. Fastening the windows more securely, Karen promised Thomas she'd get him a radio or TV as a partial replacement for the stereo.

"Wolf's getting pretty close," Thomas said, lying there with his eyes closed.

Early the next morning, I called Dave to explain the fishing trip was off.

"You mean some lowdown would steal from a guy that sick?" he said, furious and incredulous. "Well, I'll go see Thomas. He needs company, and we'll *talk* catfishing anyway."

The day continued as it had started, strenuous and discouraging. Jobs were scarce and a lot of programs that used to help people had been cut out. To do our jobs, we had to steadily produce miracles. That took more spirit than our tired staff could continuously manage. I'm sure I wasn't the only person in the office who kept finding myself praying.

That afternoon, we heard someone struggling to open our outside door. Karen wearily got up and walked over to help.

It was Dave with his arm wrapped around Thomas. Both of them were grinning at our surprise.

"I stopped right outside the door," Dave said, handing me his keys. "Could someone park my car?"

Steering Thomas to the nearest chair, Dave reminded me of a big Irish policeman, tenderly cuddling a newborn baby. Thomas was wobbly, but for the first time in days, he was smiling. We kept our hugs and greetings gentle.

"Let's go next door for a coffee party," someone suggested.

Someone dashed ahead to be sure doors were open and a chair pulled out. The rest of us helped Dave walk Thomas, with a few stops to rest along the way.

As we were getting Thomas seated at the table nearest the restaurant door, our favorite waitress rushed over. Seeing how sick he obviously was, she gave us attention worthy of Queen Elizabeth.

The kidding rarely stops at Project Return. This afternoon, it seemed even faster than usual, though somehow gentler. I was probably not the only one trying to conceal my damp eyes.

Dave quietly cut up Thomas's food, trying to save his strength in tiny ways.

"This is like my birthday all over again," Thomas said. "Hard to believe this guy used to be on death row, isn't it?" he asked, gesturing toward Dave. "We used to avoid him, thought he was a big, bad guy."

I knew from Dave's records that Thomas was telling the truth. Dave didn't seem bothered, but he did turn serious for just a moment. "Things change," he said. "Fortunately, a lot."

The laughter continued, and the gentleness.

Finally, Dave drove the car around to the restaurant door and the rest of us helped Thomas in. He was very tired by now but still smiling faintly. Dave smiled, too, and gave us an okay sign.

After they drove away, we walked back to the office, joking, solving minor problems, maybe doing a little leftover tear-shedding. Sometimes you share bread and wine, or maybe pie and coffee, and it suddenly is clear: the kingdom of God is in the midst of you.

We still needed some time off. The wolf stalking Thomas was drawing very near. But somehow our weariness was gone. Miracles don't have to be enormous.

And while they do occur often enough to keep us going, there are dry stretches in between.

A couple of weeks later, Karen and Bob conducted Thomas's funeral service in the little blue chapel at Downtown Presbyterian. In his few short free world weeks, Thomas had made a surprising number of friends and most of them were there. We sang "Nobody Knows the Trouble I've Seen" and "Amazing Grace," and buried Thomas in a graveyard his elderly aunt had chosen. Generations of black Nashvillians, some famous, have been buried there, and there was a blue autumn sky, goldenrod, and asters.

"First time I've ever seen him free," Dave said somberly, right after Bob finished that last prayer. Tears stung my eyes as I, too, imagined Thomas's glee at finding his spirit no longer earthbound.

Afterwards, we all went over to Bob's house, feeling urgently the need to be together. When Dave showed up, he'd had too much beer. We could understand it, but the alcohol worried us. That had been a cause of all his downfalls in the past.

It was a cause nearly a year later when Dave was said to have brandished a knife during a fracas in a bar. No one else was hurt. I've never understood why it was necessary to send police dogs after Dave, but he was badly bitten, with deep gashes in his legs and on his face, and one finger nearly torn off.

He'd been in jail nearly a week, with the dog bites badly infected, before we finally found a judge to order him taken to an emergency room for treatment.

If there were any way for Dave to guarantee that he would never take another drink, he would be a favorite neighbor on anyone's street. There would certainly be no point in his being sent back to prison. Not ever taking another drink is one miracle we haven't had happen very often, though—not with anyone. We'd tried with Dave, as with all the others: alcohol programs, Alcoholics Anonymous, frequent contacts, and lots of friendship. We don't give up hope, but all we've been able to do for Dave lately is stop for a chat when we're in the prison, or maybe send him a few stamps. It hurts.

It's also technically "recidivism" (which simply means being sent back to prison) and a statistical failure for Project Return. Sometimes people are returned to prison because they commit another serious crime. Sometimes they haven't committed a crime, but have failed to report to their parole officer. And sometimes, like Dave, they have done something which would have probably resulted in a short workhouse sentence if it weren't for that past record.

A low *recidivism rate* is the usual measure of success for an organization like Project Return. By that measure, we are incredibly effective; the recidivism rate I calculate is so low I wouldn't print it without years of impeccable statistics to back me up.

As corrections-related statistics go, ours are pretty accurate, probably better than those of many police or parole departments. However, like everyone else in the area, we don't really know where a lot of our people went. As far as we know, they aren't in trouble. If they were locked up in Greece or Alaska, though, we'd likely never hear about it unless they wrote to us.

Predictably, most of our Christmas cards, with pictures of new babies and news about raises and promotions, come from people who are doing well. Occasionally, there's a lonely letter or phone call from someone who's gotten locked up again, is eager to communicate good resolutions, and may need our help with a family problem, or with getting a lawyer.

We hear much faster from the occasional innocent person who is picked up by the police on suspicion. Parolees are picked up much more readily than other people, if a crime has occurred anywhere near them. This makes a certain amount of sense, but it's discouraging to a young man with a brand-new job, who's been trying really hard to do well. He may very well lose the job even if he is innocent. Someone on parole usually can't make bond, so guilty or innocent, he spends time in jail.

Obviously, we don't want our people to return to jail or prison. That's the bottom line. But the Project Return staff would never work so hard, people all over the country who are concerned about prison problems would never work so hard, simply to keep people from being locked up. What we're interested in is making real change possible.

We want our people to have a chance at happy, successful lives in the community. We want people, who have been convinced since babyhood that they have no value, to discover their infinite value. We want safe, happy communities, without victims. We want limited resources to be available for things more precious than more prison cells and police submachine guns.

Harmon Wray works for us part time doing research and development on alternatives to incarceration, and human ways we can work for the peace of our cities.

Harmon's biggest interest right now is in establishing some dispute centers where neighbors can settle their own differences without getting into expensive adversary proceedings in court. He's speaking, setting up public meetings, and having lunch with people in community organizations who are interested in trying this out.

Harmon has coordinated alternatives to prison for a couple of people, under the sponsorship of Project Return, and will probably do more of this when something extraordinary comes up. He worked with other groups to help set up the Tennessee Sentencing Support Center in Nashville, which designs alternative sentences on a much larger scale, and he works with them himself as one of the case planners.

One of the Project Return alternative programs was for John Rutherford, 78. John fatally shot a man who refused to pay back three hundred dollars he had insisted John loan him.

"What are you going to do about it?" he'd taunted, and John, tragically, showed him.

Obviously, John must never have access to a gun again. It was necessary to move him from the dangerous place where he'd been living to a neighborhood where he felt safe without the gun.

Dismas House, a halfway house we work with closely, agreed to take John in. Because his Social Security check is quite small, they also agreed to take half their usual rent and let him do extra chores for the rest. Rather than have John go to prison, they were even willing to have him live there under house arrest for the first ninety days, under orders of the court not to leave the Dismas house and yard.

Later, John was allowed to take a daily walk, and eventually to go to church on Sundays. Church had always been important to him.

Someone is dead, and that can't be changed. John's life will probably always be restricted. But, considering the possibilities, it is a good alternative. Certainly it is far better, and a great deal less expensive, than John spending the end of his life in prison.

We work continuously with people who are very much like us, although often with even less money. We laugh and cry at the same things, have similar dreams for our children, eat together sometimes, plan, and celebrate.

Then we discover that those people were brutalized as children, gang raped in prison, and spend most of their lives in a jungle we can hardly believe, even today. Some of their neighbors constantly break into their apartments and steal their possessions. It's not uncommon for them to get shot, quite casually, and sometimes it's fatal.

We've seen people we loved die, usually far too young, as a result of health problems from prison. Several people we've loved have been fatally shot.

Darlene, to whose memory I dedicated this book, was shot by mistake. She happened to be on the front porch in "the projects" when some young men were exchanging a little gunfire.

She didn't even rate an obituary in the newspaper, just one short paragraph in a story about "one more disturbance."

The day of her funeral, I received a phone call that her glasses were ready. She'd had a hopeless time in school. That was not surprising since she turned out to be almost legally blind and had severe astigmatism. She was nineteen when she died. The day before, she'd been thrilled because I had promised her that now she could finally learn to read.

Some days, it's too much. We're in no danger of "burnout," the feeling that life is lackluster and the people we work with have no value. Our jobs are never dull, but we *can* become desperate.

The only answer to that is to wait, confidently when we can manage it, for a gift. "My cup runneth over" the psalmist said, and when it finally does, there is strength and joy enough to share. Grace, when working with prisoners, often means resilience and a reliable sense of humor. It also means lying down to a good night's sleep, and taking reasonable care of your own health.

About 2,700 years before the Safe Streets Act was passed, Isaiah spelled out the task which those of us who work in the criminal justice area see as our own: "You shall be called the repairer of the breach, the restorer of streets to dwell in." That sounds a little less overwhelming when we also read the promise in the same chapter: "The Lord will guide you continually . . . and you shall be like a watered garden, like a spring of water whose waters fail not" (Isaiah 58:11-12).

◊FOR FURTHER READING◊

About Victims

Jackson, Dave, *Dial 911* (Herald Press, 1981). Peaceful Christians of Reba Place Fellowship, Evanston, Illinois, and personal encounters with crime. For older teenagers also. (Leader's Guide is available for use in group study.)

West, Jessamyn, *The Massacre at Fall Creek* (Harcourt, Brace, Jovanovich, 1975). Exciting frontier fiction illuminates one concern of people who favor the death penalty—that how much criminal is punished is indicator of how much victim was valued. For older teenagers also.

Yoder, John H., *What Would You Do?* (Herald Press, 1983). Non-violent responses when loved one is threatened. Could be used effectively with teenage group.

Zehr, Howard and Dave Jackson, *The Christian as Victim* (Mennonite Central Committee, 27 pages).

Zehr, Howard, *Who Is My Neighbor? Learning to Care for Victims of Crime* (MCC, 15 pages).

About Families and Care of Children

Erwin, John R., as told to Dell Coats Erwin, *The Man Who Keeps Going to Jail* (David C. Cook, 1978). Difficult childhood in foster homes is background for starting PACE in Cook County Jail.

Magee, Doug, *What Murder Leaves Behind: The Victim's Family* (Dodd, Mead, 1983). Sensitive anecdotal account of problems of survivors.

About Criminal Justice

American Friends Service Committee, *Struggle for Justice* (Hill and Wang, 1971). Proposals of fair and reasonable solutions to criminal justice problems.

Clark, Ramsey, *Crime in America* (Simon and Schuster, 1970). Former attorney general's humane overview of causes and effective cures for crime.

Kunen, James S., *How Can You Defend Those People?* (Random House, 1983). A young criminal lawyer encounters people simultaneously guilty and victims.

Menninger, Karl, MD, *The Crime of Punishment* (Viking Press, 1968). Everyone loses from our hodgepodge criminal justice system. World-famous psychiatrist suggests common sense improvements.

Nagel, William, *On Behalf of a Moratorium on Prison Construction.* (From the journal, *Crime and Delinquency*, 2nd quarter, 1977. Reprint available.) Nagel's lively style and surprising findings make this highly recommended reading, whether or not you usually go in for academic papers or statistics.

Silberman, Charles E., *Criminal Violence, Criminal Justice* (Vintage Books, 1980). Realistic coverage of criminal justice, with especially good interpretation of part race plays.

Wicker, Tom, *A Time to Die* (New York: Ballantine, 1975). Dramatic true story of revolt at Attica, with Wicker present as requested observer.

About Leaving Prison

Wengard, Al, *Life After Prison* (Herald Press, 1984). Life in the free world, with your family, your job, your friends, your victim, your God, and yourself. Suitable for prisoners and their close friends or family members (48 pages).

About the Death Penalty

Campbell, Will D., *The Glad River* (Holt, Rinehart, Wilson, 1982). Strong Anabaptist theme runs through this novel about the execution of one (innocent) member of small community.

Magee, Doug, *Slow Coming Dark* (Pilgrim Press, 1980). Painfully revealing interviews with Death Row prisoners.

Zehr, Howard, *Death as a Penalty* (MCC, 30 pages). Realistic reasons why the death penalty is impossible for Christians, and ineffective for anybody.

For Young People

Armstrong, William H., *Sounder* (Harper, 1969). Only the human spirit triumphant and the beautiful writing light up this story showing prison at its most brutal. Fifth grade and up.

Lee, Harper, *To Kill a Mockingbird* (J. B. Lippincott, 1960). Race and criminal justice in small Southern town in 1930s. Junior high and up.

Hickman, Martha Whitmore, *When Can Daddy Come Home?* (Abingdon, 1983). Story of prisoner's child, for children facing same experience and children learning to understand and help. For grades K-3.

Sebestyen, Ouida, *Words by Heart* (Little, Brown and Company, 1979). Black 12-year-old Lena learns painfully close-up about forgiveness and nonviolence.

Author Kit Kuperstock (left), with Nolan Eagan who, after five years in prison, was freed moments before. Nolan later worked on the staff of Project Return and is presently on the advisory committee. (Photo by Bill Welch)

◊ THE AUTHOR ◊

Kit Kuperstock is staff coordinator of Project Return, a small Nashville, Tennessee, agency that helps people finally build good futures after leaving prison.

Besides holding other jobs in the criminal justice area, she has been a newspaper reporter, magazine writer, and editor. She finally graduated from University of Tennessee after raising five sons and some foster children, and has an MPA from Tennessee State University.

Mrs. Kuperstock was born in Arkansas, and lived most of her adult life in Oak Ridge, Tennessee. She belongs to Edgehill United Methodist Church in Nashville.